D1602651

The Big Drum Ritual of Carriacou

Lorna McDaniel

The Big Drum Ritual of Carriacou

Praisesongs in Rememory of Flight

University Press of Florida

Gainesville · Tallahassee · Tampa · Boca Raton

Pensacola · Orlando · Miami · Jacksonville

03   02   01   00   99   98   6   5   4   3   2   1

Library of Congress Cataloging-in-Publication Data
McDaniel, Lorna.
The Big Drum ritual of Carriacou: Praisesongs in rememory of flight
/ Lorna McDaniel
p. cm.
Includes bibliographical references (p.) and index.
ISBN 0-8130-1607-X (cloth: alk. paper)
1. Folk music—Grenada—Carriacou Island—History and criticism.
2. Folk songs, Creole—Grenada—Carriacou Island—History and
criticism. 3. Folk dancing—Grenada—Carriacou Island. 4. Rites and
ceremonies—Grenada—Carriacou Island. 5. Carriacou Island
(Grenada)—Social life and customs. I. Title.
ML3565.M386   1998   98-13515
781.62'969729845—dc21

The University Press of Florida is the scholarly publishing agency
for the State University System of Florida, comprising Florida A&M
University, Florida Atlantic University, Florida International
University, Florida State University, University of Central Florida,
University of Florida, University of North Florida, University of
South Florida, and University of West Florida.

University Press of Florida
15 Northwest 15th Street
Gainesville, FL 32611
http://nersp.nerdc.ufl.edu/~upf

This book is performed for
Mama mwe Constance Robinson Da Costa
Papa mwe Adrian Antonio Da Costa

Contents

Figures and Tables

Figures

Tables

Acknowledgments

While I was in Carriacou, my major culture source was Sister Pearl Johns. She not only answered my questions with honesty and frankness, but taught me to plant corn in the sandy soil beside my bungalow and also, in the metaphoric English Creole language, to "plant corn-rows" in the hairstyle that imitates furrowed garden rows. She taught me coconut oil extraction, the names of fruits and herbs, and her cooking techniques. I was well fed on crab, the vegetable stew called *callaloo*, shark steak, and the traditional ground corn dish *coucou*. However, she did not succeed in warning me strongly enough against the dreadful sea egg (a sea urchin) that wounded me near the rock island Jack Adan, or of the disastrous effects of munching on a manchineel, an apple-like but poisonous beach fruit that caught my eye and almost entered my mouth.

Sister Pearl often declared that I would have plenty to tell when I returned home and that I would most remember the deep laughter that convulsed our conversations and the delight of parching nuts in sand and toasting ground corn (to be mixed with sugar to make the snack food known as asham) over our "three-stone" fire.

From our first meeting when she was called by "old head" Sugar Adams to meet with me, my chief source of song material was Lucian Duncan, a powerful, affecting *chantwell* (lead singer/dancer). I frequently interviewed Lucian at her hilltop Mount Royal home, recording her songs and taking pictures of dance types. I questioned her on ritual form, spiritual thought, and on the meaning of the Patois texts I had taped at several Big Drum performances.

Through Lucian I met Jones "Pofella" Corion, who at eighty-eight offered me samples of his favorite genre, a valuable group of songs called the Halle-cord. Estimie Andrews, leader of the Big Drum ensemble, the Carriacou Cultural Organization, introduced me to the Patois culture in her L'Esterre rum shop where men gathered to play dominos, drink, and talk; Ophelia Mundi opened her home to me so that I could witness the family ancestral tribute, the *saraca*. Peter Benjamin, violinist and quadrille expert, helped me with Patois meanings and also involved me in his work with young string players, encouraging their appreciation of quadrille music and dance. Sister Clemmie Quashie Hazel, owner of my seafront cottage outside the town of Hillsborough, reminisced about her father, Adolphus Quashie, and was also a tremendous source of encouragement in my work.

Father Colbert Lewis, with whom I worked as organist at the Anglican church of Christ the King, was especially supportive of my work. He permitted me to peruse baptismal records, which I used to establish subjects in the Big Drum songs and to search for the approximate dates of the songs. He also encouraged an Emancipation Day Mass in which the Big Drum Patois texts were transformed by Lucian Duncan and Pofella Corion for use in the service. I was able to glean from this creative effort (which was coordinated by young people of the church and myself) the attitudes of the congregation toward the dance ritual as a religious form and also concepts on composition from a performer's point of view.

My introduction to Paule Marshall's novel *Praisesong for the Widow*, which inspired this research, came from my amazing sister-in-law Patricia Da Costa, whose keen sensibilities have always been a dependable guide. My brother, Noel Da Costa, copied the original musical transcriptions and offered guidance on transcription problems; Theodora Moorehead read much of the preliminary manuscript; and my son, Dill, furnished the reassurance needed. They all offered emotional and familial support throughout every phase of this work, and financial support during the crisis days—my short flight to Union Island in October 1983 at the peak of the Grenada Revolutionary Army's attack on the people. This internal conflict grew to international proportions outlined in chapter 4.

My early studies were enhanced by research in Trinidad funded by a Fulbright grant in 1988, work in Tobago in 1989, and studies at the Smithsonian on a short-term visitor's grant in 1993. During my study year in Trinidad and Tobago, Jean Pearse, widow of Andrew Pearse, not only permitted me to peruse the Pearse archives but also generously hosted me for two months in her home. Donald Hill also shared materials from his extensive ethnography with me in refreshingly collaborative ways, and his support improves this publication. Early on, however, my dissertation adviser, Carol Robertson, had

1. Culture bearers. *Clockwise from top left:* Sister Pearl Johns, Peter Benjamin, Ophelia Mundi, Zeea Allert, Marian St. John, Pofella Corion.

structured an experimental arena for me out of which these discussions are taken. Her methods continue as my model and her work as the chief source in the formation of my academic ideal.

Several friends, culture bearers, and scholars who offered major contributions to this study are listed here: Augustus Adams, Janus Adams, Zea Allert, "Nennen" Alexis, "Gentle" and Olina Andrews, Roy Benjamin, Hector Blair, Frances Brinkley, Bernard Bullen, Glenna Bullen, Wendell Bullen, the Bethel family, Wally Bethel, "Welcome" Clements, Donna Corion, "Welcome" Cummings, Grantis "The Lion" Cudjo, Simeon Cudjo, Nanette de Jong, Nina De Voe, Obinkaram Echewa, Alfred George, Misler George, Archbishop Edmund Gilbert, Maxman Joseph, David Lambert, Prince Lawrence, Myrl Lewis, Barbara Poindexter, Ali Pollack, George Prime, Muriel Roberts, the Samerson family, Gertrude Simon, Henrietta Simon, Florence Snagg, "Mama" Steele, Marian St. John, Peggy Thamm, Rt. Rev. Eudora Thomas, Carl Michael Vaulx, Genevieve Weber, Lise Winer, Linda Williams, Phyllis Wynn. Special thanks go to Carriacou violinist/painter Canute Caliste for his paintings and to photographer Chester Higgins for his award-winning cover photo of the Carriacou Cultural Organization.

My thanks go to editor-in-chief Meredith Morris-Babb for "taking a chance" on this internal history and to project editor Judy Goffman, who managed the unwieldy task of differentiating the multiple languages and orthographies in the Creole texts.

I hope this study reflects the attitude of my culture bearers in honoring historical memory, a memory that also inspired the deceased "old parent" drummers—Sugar Adams, Titus Lambert, Williamson Lambert, Heinze Lambert, and Daniel Aikens—and dancers—May Fortune Adams, Collie Lendore, Rachel John, Drina George, Se Misela, Se Gol, and Se Adelaide.

The Big Drum Ritual of Carriacou

Introduction

> Her body she always usta say might be in Tatem but
> her mind, her mind was long gone with the Ibos.
>
> Paule Marshall, *Praisesong for the Widow*

Paule Marshall's elegant novel *Praisesong for the Widow* directed
my discovery of Carriacou's ancestral ritual, the Big Drum. Despite my previous awareness of a large body of ethnographic material on the island, it was
Marshall's book, published in 1983, that inspired my interest in the musical
traditions of Carriacou.

The novel is filled with familiar references to African-American music and
culture; blues verses, jazz dances, and quotes from the poetry of Langston
Hughes adorn the narrative. The author's reliance on African-American cultural themes convinced me that her references to the Big Drum were not fic-
tive and that the French-named Caribbean dances introduced near the end of
the book had been as carefully researched as the opening section. If Carriacou's musical culture was as rich and distinctive as Marshall portrayed, the
tiny island would make a perfect research site for a dissertation project. I set
out for Grenada to trace the passage of the novel's protagonist and ended up
finding on the island an active tradition, people who call themselves African, a
wealth of musical and linguistic survivals, and a multilayered event that integrates song, ensemble drumming, and dance.

During my first visit to Carriacou in April 1983, "old head" culture bearer

Gentle Andrews recited a traditional legend to me. He told it this way: "The Africans who were brought here did not like it. They just walked to the sea. They all began to sing as they spread their arms. A few rose to the sky. Only those who did not eat salt left the ground. The Africans flew home." This was an encapsulated variation of a tale, "The Igbo Landing," that I had read in the Marshall novel. Taking this coincidence and also the lively, open rapport that developed between the Carriacou dancers and drummers and me as positive signs, I decided to study the Big Drum.

When I returned to Carriacou in September 1983, I became increasingly interested in the story and especially in Marshall's sources. I have since learned that the tale was taken from *Drums and Shadows* of the Georgia Writers' Project, in which culture bearers' interpretations of the story are recorded as a historical event that took place on St. Simons Island or as a transcendent spiritual return to Africa. I went on to gather several variants of the story from oral recitations and published literature on the Caribbean as well as from sources on Georgia and South Carolina culture. The wide distribution of the tale implies a depth of cultural sharing among Africans throughout the diaspora, a unified experience, a profound longing for Africa. The story is at once a segment of history, a tale founded upon factual experience, and a myth formulated from the longing for freedom and the desire to return to the homeland. I call the incorporated tale/myth "The Flying Africans."

Marshall's version of the tale is a retrieved childhood memory of an African-American woman named Avatara "Avey" Johnson. Her secondhand memory, passed down by her great-aunt Cuney, is full of images that are difficult for a child to cope with—indelible fragments of history—of enslaved people walking into the water at Igbo Landing. She tries to erase the painful story from her mind. However, during a cruise to Grenada the moribund information surfaces, as interpretable signs, unconscious messages and dreams—much valued in Caribbean cultural practice. Confused by the appearance of her great-aunt Cuney in a dream, Avey abandons her tour group and plans an early and solitary return home.

Awaiting her return flight, she goes for a walk on the beach. Overwhelmed by the sun and her own inner reflections, she takes shelter in a dark rum shop. She meets the owner, Lebert Joseph, who notices her confusion and befriends her. He also sees in her a deeper anxiety, and like the uneven-legged Legba of Dahomean religions he guides her to Carriacou, to the Big Drum, and to a rememory of her Aunt Cuney's story. At his insistence she boards a hand-hewn schooner for a rough four-hour journey from Grenada to Carriacou, "re-experiencing" the horrible, saline nausea of the Middle Passage. After episodes of seasickness and vomiting she is nursed back to health by Lebert Joseph's daughter and given a bath, symbolic of a ritual spiritual cleansing.

As planned, the limping old man, the gatekeeper of knowledge, meets her at the crossroads to escort her to the time-honored festival of dance, song, and drumming, the Big Drum. The event unleashes an awareness in her: a familiarity with dance, language, and music; a recognition of the triangular relationship in the African diaspora (the connectedness of Africa, the Caribbean, and South Carolina); a re-memory of history, nation, and name.

Praisesong for the Widow envelops a grand travel metaphor of personal transformation brought about by the sudden insight and the reflection of Africa in the musical forms and dances created by the wanderings of Africans. Marshall's novel suggests that knowledge imposes duty—the duty to remember and perpetuate the sensibilities acquired by the "journey."

Several re-creations of the "The Flying Africans" have recently sprung from African-American writers who have incorporated the theme of flight in their fiction. Contemporary black female novelists Maryse Condé, Jamaica Kincaid, Toni Cade Bambara, and Toni Morrison (in *Song of Solomon*) have alluded to mysterious corporal displacement or have integrated the myth in culturally telling ways. Poet Robert Hayden (in "Middle Passage" and "O Daedalus, Fly Away Home") uses the theme as well. Joseph Zobel's novel *La Rue Cases-Negres*, which inspired the film *Sugar Cane Alley*, *Sankofa*, directed by Euzhan Palcy; a film by Julie Dash, *Daughters of the Dust*, Virginia Hamilton's children's book *The People Could Fly*, and Earl Lovelace's novel *Salt*, relate the same story. The tale is thus being passed on to even larger audiences. The new telling is also being performed as visual art (a University of Pennsylvania exhibit, "High Flying"), and on stage accompanied by music. Wendell Logan, professor of music at Oberlin College, has prepared an orchestral piece based on the march at Igbo Landing. The Christian vision of heavenly ascent permeates the spiritual and hymnody of the black church (see McDaniel 1990), and from these songs, gospel, popular, reggae, and rap musicians revive the message. Examples are "I'll Fly from Here" (Mavis Staples), "I Believe I Can Fly" (R. Kelly), "Rasta Man Chant" (Bob Marley), and "I'll Be Missing You" (Puff Daddy). Along with this major new dissemination through composers, filmmakers, and authors, the story is still remembered in Georgia, South Carolina, Brazil, and the Caribbean by elders who tell it with total conviction as their parents told it.

To discover social meaning in the Big Drum texts, I superimpose on my research the myth (or reality) of flight as a historical, spiritual, and aesthetic metaphor. I use the several interpretations of "The Flying Africans" as signposts to direct the musical elements under analysis. Four levels of flight are sketched in my analysis: the rebellious, physical flight from enslavement—and its final flight in suicide; the artistic, dream-inspired flight of the ritual dance; the spiritual flight of religious ecstasy; and the compositional flight that creates a historical musical legacy. These interpretations of flight and focus are submerged in the four chapters, which are titled after the chapters in *Praisesong for the Widow*. By this device I extend homage to Paule Marshall.

The title of chapter 1, "The Runagate Nation," was borrowed from Marshall, who in turn used the title "Runagate" from Robert Hayden's poem in which he portrays the fear of a slave runagate in the desperation of "elopement." Here I explore the oldest songs in the Big Drum repertoire, songs from the era when the deepest desire was to escape. Juxtaposing the oral song texts with written colonial documents, I trace the origins of the people and the interactions between national groups and also interpret the people's decisions either to accommodate or rebel.

In chapter 2, "Sleepers Awake!" I employ the Creole cycle of songs to interpret dream-inspired and aesthetic resolutions in the imagination of flight. In chapter 3, "Lavé Tete," I compare the Big Drum to other Caribbean rituals in which possession is practiced, incorporating an overview of the major Caribbean rituals, the less prominent ancestral rites, and the "invented tradition" (Hobsbawm), the Rastafarian religion. Through linguistic connections, I draw a literary paradigm that may help illuminate the mysterious aspects of possession and dance.; and in chapter 4, "Beg Pardon," I analyze techniques of composition in the Big Drum, relating them to modern calypso. The Mighty Sparrow's calypso song "Grenada" is used to outline the politics and people's reaction to the Grenada invasion as well as to connect the musical function of calypso with the Bélè "Great Event" songs of protest in the Big Drum ritual.

These four chapters, based upon four ideals of flight, are strengthened by comparative research notes and excerpts from historical documents, which may be used for further analysis.

The song, ritual, and dance metaphors of the Big Drum, created by enslaved people, should be understood as signifying "languages" that, because of the nature of slave society, store deeply controlled desires and covert interactions. Interpretation of their new languages in the form of this formidable cache of personal testimonies (129 songs), and 32 dances, permits us to encounter individual and social choices of the song owners and illuminate the responses of people to bondage.

Along with the personal testimonies and songs I have drawn on the sparse collection of documents from the past written by those in power whose purpose was control. These documents reveal fear, cloaked in dominance and expressed through exercises in mental torment and physical abuse.

Some years ago, Sidney Mintz called attention to the avoidance by researchers of cognitive orientations active below the level of consciousness and the lack of ethnographic studies involving interpersonal style. He wrote, "This neglect has less to do with the importance such concepts ought to have in cultural description than with the poverty of our conceptual tools" (1976:6). Two years later Kay Shelemay suggested an approach called historical ethnomusicology, in which musical materials were employed to discover history. She described the possibilities this way:

> The potential of the ethnomusicological contribution to historical reconstruction rests with the richness of our materials. These materials, including both music and ritual complexes of which it may be a part, are primary cultural documents within which crucial evidence is encoded. . . . Hence an ethnomusicological study of living music culture provides a multi-faceted and unique data base, which in its totality may well illuminate important aspects of a culture's history. (1980:234)

This study utilizes the research method proposed by Shelemay and, I hope, will help fill the gap suggested by Mintz. Not only do I examine cultural documents (the living "languages"—song, ritual, and dance), I also struggle with etymologies to wrest from them clues that might communicate the ethos of a former time and offer insight into the complex racial, religious, and cultural integrations that gave birth to new peoples and Creole languages in the "new world." In this way, and with the aid of recorded history, I read historical attitudes and beliefs through the coded musical languages and ritual practices of the Big Drum. My objective is to decode the surviving ancient symbols of sound, text, movement, and behavior, to define the social world of the Africans who were newly transplanted, and to present not just their anthropology but also their history, sentiments, and inner convictions.

While researchers sit in Caribbean "yards" awaiting culture bearers' responses to unanswerable questions, new history is always being made. In 1983, as I sought understanding in ancient songs of alienation and protest, a surreal drama of military prowess was taking place not far from my culture bearer's home. A week after the U.S. invasion of Grenada on October 17, Carriacou was invaded.

The largest of the Grenadines, that chain of rock islands linking Grenada and St. Vincent, Carriacou measures only 7½ by 3½ miles. More than 6,000 people make their homes there, and thousands more live and work in London, New York, and Toronto. Like its neighbor Petit Martinique, Carriacou is governed by Grenada.

The bungled U.S. invasion sparked interest in Grenada and introduced the name of Carriacou to the general public, though many still confuse the island with Curaçao. Even before the secretive military invasion, to which the media were not invited, the fame of the tiny island, at least among social scientists, far exceeded its minute proportions.

M. G. Smith's discovery of the islanders' unusual system of patrilineality, reported in 1962 in *Kinship and Community in Carriacou*, attracted the interest of anthropologists. Carriacou's deep social continuities captivated ethnographers, historians, dance ethnologists, linguists, and other social scientists. The late Andrew Pearse was first among those who, in the early 1950s, extensively recorded and studied the Big Drum. Though much of Pearse's work remains unpublished, his initial dance classifications and research are incorporated here, as are his founding assumptions about the African basis of the oral literature. His inspired appreciation of the wealth of the song literature informs my work throughout. I hope that this interpretation will be regarded as a continuation of his work.

Also fundamental to my study is Donald Hill's two-volume dissertation, "England I Want To Go: The Impact of Migration on a Caribbean Community"; his monograph, *The Impact of Migration on the Metropolitan and Folk Society of Carriacou, Grenada*; and his recording, *The Big Drum and Other Ritual and Social Music of Carriacou*.

Others who have sought out Carriacou as a research site include Pearl Primus, Percival Borde, Bruce Procope, J. D. Elder, Annette Macdonald, Alan

Lomax, Argeliers Leon, Rolando Fernandez, Olavo Alen, Laura Vilar, Ron Kephart, and Beth Mills and indigenous researchers W. A. Redhead, Frances Brinkley, Christine David, and Winston Fleary.

As an Antiguan-born African American of Jamaican parentage, my methods and behavior in other people's "yards" differ from those suggested in fieldwork manuals. So, too, do my conclusions contradict many of the model studies cited in my bibliography. At the same time, I embrace the early studies, which were essential to my arrival at this stage in my work.

I have had to adjust my thinking over time, however, for I work in a discipline that continues to evolve away from a pure Eurocentric outlook, from a stance of distancing that harbors a quaint perception of the "Other," to a position that listens at closer range. As an ethnic researcher within a society self-consciously representing a "double-consciousness" (W. E. B. DuBois) and "double-voicedness" (Henry Louis Gates), and aware of the duality because of my own social experiences, I experiment here with transposing the "tonality" of my voice. Despite my efforts to write a work devoid of exploitative techniques, an analysis that includes rather than excludes, that shares "authority" and that incorporates the voice of the culture bearer, I have arrived at selections by deciding which of them move *me*, which of them tell *my* history. In this text I locate myself as "insider" or "outsider" alternately depending on the discussion.

In certain circumstances the ethnic researcher who declares herself a member of the society under scrutiny may indeed occupy a special place in that society. She may more easily become part of the social structure and thereby, as Lévi-Strauss suggests, occupy a "favoured position" or hold a "personal advantage" (1983:xvi). However, in on-site research all scholars occupy some level between "outsider" and "insider," assigned by segments of the society in response to the researcher's phenotype, class, culture, country of origin, or attitude. Normally one is typed by conditions or alliances that are beyond the researcher's control, that are braided into the history of the society.

Shortly after the 1992 Los Angeles rebellion, Toni Morrison commented to the predominantly white graduating class at the University of Michigan on the power of history:

> History can be critiqued and analyzed—artists can reinvent it. . . . It can deliver other information and insights. [The rewriting of history

is] the urgent enterprise when blood and rage bubbles in the streets . . . [for] the past can be more liberating if you can change its lies . . . [projecting] the brightest of the future and also the best of the past.

And here is the pungent piece of history, the expression of longing for homeland and repatriation that Aunt Cuney passed on to Avey, that inspired my interpretation of the Big Drum:

> It was here that they brought 'em. They taken 'em out of the boats right here where we's standing. Nobody remembers how many of 'em it was, but they was a good few 'cording to my gran' who was a little girl no bigger than you when it happened. The small boats was drawed up here and the ship they had just come from was out in the deep water. Great big ol' ship with sails. And the minute those Ibos was brought on shore they just stopped, my gran' said, and taken a look around. A good long look. Not saying a word . . . they just turned . . . all of them . . . and walked on back down to the edge of the river here. . . . They just kept walking right on out over the river. . . . When they realized there wasn't nothing between them and home but some water and that wasn't giving 'em no trouble they got so tickled they started to singing. They sounded like they was having such a good time my gran' declared she just picked herself up and took off after 'em. In her mind. Her body she always usta say might be in Tatem but her mind, her mind was long gone with the Ibos. (Marshall 1983: 38)

The Musical Transcriptions

I hope that culture bearers in Carriacou will be interested in reading this history despite my insistence on using the musical sketches that are distributed throughout. They had coldly warned me early on, when I enthusiastically and, as I thought at the time, generously promised to notate their songs, that they "did not read music." Their signifyin' statement sunk in only much later, when I realized that what they were implying was that the transcriptions were for me, not them.

Transcriptions help ethnomusicologists project the musical elements and their distinctive characteristics. Here they do not represent the actual sounds.

They are not meant nor should they be expected to describe the tonal structure in its broad substance. I assume that some musical elements escape the ear, and conversely that the ear may recognize lines not actually sounded by any of the individual musicians. On the other hand, the eye can sometimes distinguish interlocking, overlapping parts lost to the ear.

Though too slowly, anthropologists and ethnologists have begun to question their manipulation and distortion of musical "facts" and their disregard for the subtleties of "other people's music." Still, perhaps because of a bias in favor of Western music in their training, ethnomusicologists remain preoccupied with melody. Even here, the boldly improvised drum statement, too complex to transcribe, is relegated to a mere verbal description. We continue to force squares into circles in constructing musical transcriptions that emphasize something other than the actual complexity of the sound. In transcribing only the vocal line and texts, we flagrantly ignore the multimetric drumming; this is only because it is very difficult to chart the interlocking designs on paper. To remind us of our lapses, I insert a new clef into these transcriptions. Instead of the treble clef I will use what I call the "cyclephonic clef," which indicates the texture and primacy of the improvised solo drum line.

The most essential and idiosyncratic elements of the Big Drum—voice timbre, musical approach, improvisational feel, ensemble texture, and rhythmic concord—are characteristics not duplicable in our notation system, and because of this there are often inaccuracies in transcriptions of African-type musical forms. Some of the Big Drum songs transcribed here comprise a skeletal two measures of notation, simply a few notes with an indication of a repeated pattern. In performance, however, the two measures may expand into a fleshed-out and deeply complex 15 minute performance. Also omitted here are the sophisticated stylistic features of attack, phrase delay, and embellishment in vocal approach, along with the ineffable multilinear patterns in the music.

Readers should understand that this multilinear texture is the central focus of the Big Drum. In addition, the sheet of background sound produced by the vocally responsive audience, interjecting "ai, dancer!" "ai, drummer!" "good, gal!" and "take ya time!" mixed with raucous laughter, frame and enliven the musical statements.

For ethnomusicologists, notating this multi-metered rhythmic concord will remain an unnerving challenge and will end up revealing, at best, more about the researcher's attitudes and assumptions than about the music itself.

Indications of repetition should not be taken literally as an exact duplica-
tion of the statement. In the cyclic patterning, every line in some structural or
musical way is distinct from all others. I have coined the term *cyclephonic*
to describe this multi-part texture combined with repeated vocal call-and-
response cycles, where repetitions are varied, causing shifting textural con-
cords and alternate points of tension and release in each statement.

In figure 2, the initial song statement fills the outer circle of the cyclephonic spiral diagram and the second loop indicates a repetition with choral
response. The inner coils represent the consecutive entrances of the boula
drums, the cutter drum, and finally the dance. Points of entry may differ at
each performance and with the length of the song, but the progression of en-
tries in the exposition is strictly observed.

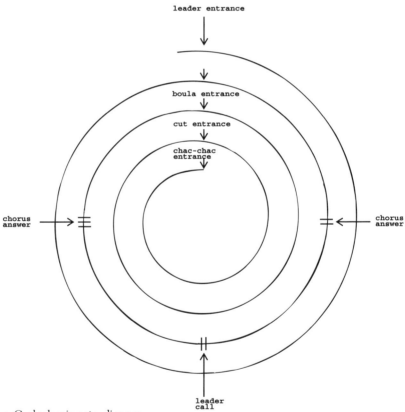

2. Cyclephonic entry diagram.

A representation of the cyclephonic spiral is used as a clef to indicate the G line and also as an indication of the African-type multilinear texture, cyclic form, and improvisational nature of this music. Figure 3 diagrams the notion of cyclic texture.

 3. Cyclephonic clef sign.

Language Performance

Three independent languages, French Creole, Standard English, and English Creole, are spoken in Carriacou. The culture is not truly trilingual, however, because French Creole, derived from French and several African languages, is rapidly disappearing. It continues among a very few older residents and among middle-aged folk only as a point of conscious cultural continuity. Most young people dismiss the language completely, while their parents blame the oldest generation for not sharing it because it was precious to them as a secret code language.

Varieties of French Creole (called Patois by Carriacouans) are spoken in St. Lucia, Dominica, Martinique, Guadeloupe, St. Barthelemy, St. Martin, Haiti, French Guiana, Mauritius, Seychelles, and in some parts of and to varying extents in Louisiana, Grenada, Petite Martinique, and Carriacou. As many linguists have shown, Patois is an independent language and not, as Carriacouans often declare, "broken French."

Patois has a highly codified grammar with sentences characterized by explicit rules that differ, of course, from French grammatical patterns. This is merely another way of saying that Patois is a language distinct from French, and although it shares part of the same sound system and vocabulary, Patois meanings diverge fundamentally from those of its source languages. Despite the similarities in French and Patois, they are not mutually intelligible (Valdman 1970:6).

Because contemporary Carriacou Patois speakers employ the language primarily to engage in pleasantries and private talk, it continues to drift, producing inconsistencies, especially in vowel sounds. Vowels may alternate in individual speech and between the speech patterns of two competent speakers. For example, the long canvas bag used in former times for gathering cotton may be pronounced "jula" or "jola." *Judi,* meaning "today," may sound like "jodi."

The bilingualism of the culture has been sharply debated by Wilfred Redhead, a former chief official of Carriacou, and M. G. Smith (D. Hill 1974:130). Redhead took the position that Carriacouans were not fluent Patois speakers. Smith incorrectly assumed their knowledge of Patois because of the centrality of Patois in the Big Drum and the wide participation of the people in the Big Drum events. In the twenty years since the dispute was aired Patois usage has declined to easily discernible and verifiable levels. In 1984 I was able to identify only ten competent Patois speakers in the L'Esterre community, in contrast to Smith's 163 in a 1953 L'Esterre population of 175. This huge discrepancy may have resulted from my adherence to a strict definition of "language competence" that was not brought into the question earlier and that is, in any case, evaluative and subjective. But a precipitous drop in the number of speakers of Patois has undoubtedly occurred.

In the past the island was linguistically sectioned, with the creolized languages spoken in the "French" area among the Belmont and L'Esterre populations, the "English" variation spoken in the central part of the island, and the "Scottish" in the northern areas. Often differences in opinion grow out of abstracted research that ignores the subtle linguistic variations over the entire island.

Language used in conjunction with music may change in structure, grammar, phonetics, and function. Language set to music need not be literal or even understandable; new and symbolic meanings may be added to archaic phrases (Merriam 1964:189). Texts and vocables incomprehensible to the society itself may even be used.

Spellings vary due to the capricious oral origins of the materials, variations in the orthographies used by individual researchers, the wide range in the age of the research documents, and the influence of the Patois languages of Haiti and St. Lucia. The comparative textual examples used here are taken from the work of Donald Hill, M. G. Smith, Andrew Pearse, Harold Courlander, and Melville Herskovits and are quoted in their original forms. Where Smith uses *fa me* for *famil* and Hill writes *sa memba guy* for *sa meme bagay,* the notations are interpretations of a particular language ideal and as such carry great weight and meaning.

The transcriptions of earlier scholars were essential guides during my slow trek into the language forest, which in Carriacou has no written glossary, only memory and personal definitions. More than this, the transcriptions simply comprise the debate—and controversy—surrounding Patois orthography. I have decided to stay close to the older song texts in order to make my points by analogy and to foster consistency in the research on Carriacou. I use the admittedly antique system embraced by Andrew Pearse—a Laubach-based orthography. Pearse presents it this way: "Each letter has one sound only. All sounds are in English except:

a	(as in bar)
i	(as in need)
g	(as in get)
j	(as in measure)
u	(as in o in move)
o'	(as in not)
e'	(as in day)
e<	(as in let)

Nasalization is indicated by the a, e, and o (circumflexed)" (1956:3). This traditional, nasal pronunciation is virtually lost in modern performances from which my transcriptions are taken; however, I emphasize the historical contexts of the Patois songs by stressing the lexicon root of the language. A few words retain French spellings merely to underscore their derivation, but only when the Patois pronunciation does not radically differ from the French.

Carriacou speech is ornamented by brief proverbs—elegant, condensed understatements of straightforward truths born of experience. The following proverbs offer attitudinal statements on the nature of language:

1. Lang neg c'est lian. (The tongue of a black person is like a whip.)
2. Big words don't know his master a small man.
3. Open mouth—words fall out.
4. Sense make before book.
5. All food is good food to eat, but all words is not good to talk.

All words may not be good to talk if there is evil intent, but there is, on the whole, pleasure to be had in Carriacou conversation, for dialogue and storytelling excite the gathering, calm the mourner, and bond and bring hope and humor to the community. The Nancy tales, now seldom heard, served this function and were an important element in wake and prayer-meeting rituals for the dead. These stories are built around animal tales from the same genre as the North American tales of Uncle Remus and the Ti Malice stories of Haiti. The spelling varies from *Annancy, Ananci, Anansi,* and *Anancy* to *Nancy,* but its origin is the Twi word for spider, *ananse* (Cassidy 1961:275). From the Patois word for spider, *zanguien,* they are also called the Zien or Czien stories (Delzin 1977). Here M. G. Smith describes a Nancy storytelling setting he presumably experienced:

> The cycle of Nancy stories is widespread throughout the Caribbean and has clear West African origins and inspiration, Anancy himself having a Kromanti—that is, Akan—name. Besides these Anancy stories, other animal stories are recited at Carriacou funeral rites.
>
> Each tale is preceded by a patois song, the storyteller singing the theme as he hops into the ring, while the audience responds in chorus, clapping their hands at the narrator's gestures. This continues until a vigorous rapport has been established; then the storyteller abruptly discontinues his singing with the cry "Crick!" to which the audience replies "Crac!" as he plunges into his tale. (1962a:155)

Tales may be told in English, Patois, or a mixture of the two. Often such language interpolations produce stories in themselves, with new meanings, new songs, or utter confusion. Captain Paul Mitchell, a veteran seaman, left behind several tales and proverbs of his own that still circulate in his village, L'Esterre. This one illustrates the chaos that sometimes arises in a culture with a multi-language history.

> Someone stole Baba's sheep. The thief pleaded "not guilty" in the court. Baba, in his funny speech said to the judge: "I had my ship (sheep) tied pon (upon) de pan' (pond)." (The thief heard "pan," which in Patois means "to hang.") He interrupted: "Gadé, mwe tan zo ka parlé con pan. Si zo ka dijé, dijé bien. Ba volè bef, c'est youn petit mutton meg mwe pwe" (Look, me hear you talk 'bout hang. When you go judge, judge right. Ent no cow, one little meager sheep me tak). (E. Andrews 1984)

The etymology of words provides an essential key to the ideas they symbolize, which in turn clarifies the formation of an evolved concept. Words, and their derivatives and parallel language translations, connect and thicken symbols. Consequently, the layering of language with double meanings, alternative contextual meanings, and signifying constructs leads to deeper explanations of a word or a cultural concept. An understanding of language relationships, language attitudes, and etymologies is essential to the difficult problem of interpretation when texts are, as in the Big Drum oral program, fragmented, in a mixed-language form, and functioning with attenuated original meanings.

Furthermore, ritual languages like African "Langage" in the Grenadian Shango ritual, Spiritual Baptist ecstatic glossolalia, and the "speaking in tongues" of the various possession societies exist throughout the Caribbean. These languages operate in a realm where mystical powers of inspired speech and song are nurtured and considered gifts acquired through revelation during trance or power (possession) states.

While religious trance is rarely a part of the Big Drum drama and the structure of the Big Drum ensemble is not institutionalized as are those of church organizations, there is an exclusivity and authority acquired through the knowledge of its coded language. Big Drum texts are in some ways akin to the language of possession: there is a guardedness surrounding their transmission and interpretation and the song words are not part of everyday discourse. Still they live on. For example, Estimie Andrews once delightfully recalled for me the difficulty she had in preserving a song text by having a child "capture" it by learning it from a knowledgeable but in this instance a reluctant elder. The child returned knowing all but one line, requiring a second trip (and a pint of rum for the elder as payment).

One

The Runagate Nation

... and when shall I reach that somewhere
morning and keep on going and never turn
back and keep on going
          Runagate
                    Runagate
                              Runagate

—Robert Hayden, "Runagate Runagate"

Some people participate in multi-vocal spiritual dances, variously
known as cults, rituals, or religions, simply for the pleasure of wheeling, jump-
ing, and "mashing" the earth, while others partake of the ecstasy in movement. Still others obtain contact with deities and ancestors through the
mental entrainment of rhythm. In the past, especially under slavery, people
choreographed complex and deeply felt meditations. As we explore interpretations of ritual languages, we assume that dance itself maps a "route of travel
and translation" (Clifford 1997).

Jerome Handler and Charlotte Frisbie lament that the limited historical literature on Barbados does not provide sufficient clues to discern to the true nature of the music of enslaved people (1972:7). Similarly, M. G. Smith has stated that "we have no information from this period [the era of slavery] about the way in which Carriacou slaves differentiated themselves" (1962a:59). Through a study of the Big Drum we can correct this, at least for Carriacou. The Big Drum offers not only music but also a body of societal evidence replete with textual, dance-related, and musical detail, formed in the historical voice of the people and encompassing significant aspects of the people's social history.

Today Carriacouans participate in the Big Drum to express their relationship with the past and their adoration of another world; through this avid attention to the past they express a compressed sense of boundaries and time. The sea that restrained their foreparents has never shackled their imaginations. Their sense of the past has created, through the dance ritual, a significant social mechanism that permeates modern interpersonal behavior.

The dance dramas survive as invisible libretti written in unknown languages—languages for which glossaries were never created. The historical oral texts deserve elucidation for they are almost miraculously preserved, from multiple sources that supplicate international gods or that invoke the people's own ancestors.

When the Big Drum began is not known, but the oldest songs of the repertoire incorporate texts concerning the period of slavery. We may assume, then, that it had evolved well before 1838, the year slavery ended in the British Caribbean. Although the texts are sung in a French Creole, the songs were not necessarily composed during the French colonial period (from 1650 to 1763). Languages are not so easily truncated. Until comparatively recent times Patois was widely used, and it was spoken throughout the more than two hundred years of British rule over the island. Patois persisted during the hostile period after the British takeover in 1763, the retrieval by France in 1779, and the final restoration again to England in 1783 through the Treaty of Versailles (Steele 1974:10).

But the vernacular did not remain impervious to the lengthy British governance. Patois was restricted to more and more confined circles throughout the British colonial period. It continued through emancipation in 1838 and into the twentieth century but lost its hold on the people during the modern period, which saw Grenada achieve independence in 1974, undergo a Marxist revolution in 1979, and endure an American invasion in 1983. As of the late 1990s, fewer than ten people on Carriacou were fluent speakers of Patois pleasantries. However, in the Big Drum Carriacou preserves its rich though fragmented Patois poetry, which entreats, summons, petitions, and dialogues with voices of the past. Sprinkled within the praise/poetry of the oldest songs are a few African words, place names such as *Dahomey* and *Kongo*, and the names of deities and ancestors.

The people of the Big Drum preserve texts that project meanings different from those understood by their foremothers and forefathers. They no longer recall specific ancestors but instead relate a rich, tenacious legacy of a collective African past. Lost meanings are not found in the French Larousse or in African-language dictionaries. As a whole, this repository relates a deeper meaning than literal translations (if they were available) would bring out.

The Big Drum evening event comprises the mingled, transformed, and evolved national dance repertoires of the West African people who were brought to Carriacou during slavery. The Nation songs and dances are the oldest items in the dance program, and at one time they were the only dances in the ritual. They were classified by the old parents themselves and kept distinct in nine types, representing the West African origins of Carriacouans: Cromanti, Igbo, Manding, Kongo, Arada, Moko, Chamba, Temne, and Banda. In recognition of the discrete multinational core repertoire, the ceremony was, and sometimes is even now, referred to as the Nation dance.

Andrew Pearse has described two other subdivisions that were accreted onto the ancient core of dances—Creole dances and Frivolous dances. Though Pearse's list appears at first glance to reflect dances of three separate eras, the classification system in fact considers the Nation group a distinctive, primarily sacred genre, the Creole group for the most part is secular, and the Frivolous group as a set of borrowed and imported dances (Pearse n.d.) appropriated in the culturally assigned cycle of Carriacouan migrations.

Dance Classifications

The Nation group appended syncretized styles such as the Scotch Chamba and Scotch Kongo; the Creole group absorbed the Quelbe (Boula), Bongo Sorti, and the Dama. The Piké, also called Shove Along, was imported from Grenada; the Chattam came from Antigua; and the Cariso, Man Bongo, and

Kalenda were appropriated from Trinidad. Union Island contributed the Ladderis (which may have been a form of the Cheerup), the Quelby (Boula), and the Lora (Pearse 1978–79:638). I add the Woman Kalenda to the Frivolous group, in which it and the Cheerup, Piké, Man Bongo, and Trinidad Kalenda survive (see table 1).

The contemporary Big Drum commemorates the major life events of individuals, families, and the community. Open affairs such as a wedding, a boat launching, the dedication of a new house, the "stone feast" (the deceased person's final burial), the memorial of a death, the Shango hair cutting (to ward off danger threatening a child), and the sacrifice/maroon offering made to the gods and ancestors for their goodwill and sustenance, present opportunities for performance. The event may also be performed as a cultural concert for tourists, a political celebration, or a regatta show.

Table 1. Big Drum dance classifications

Nation	Creole	Frivolous
Cromanti	Old Bongo	Chattam
Arada	Hallecord	Lora
Chamba	Bélè Kawé	Cariso
Manding	Gwa Bélè	Chirrup (Cheer up)
Congo	Old Kalenda	Piké
Banda	Juba	Chiffoné
Igbo		Man Bongo
Jig Igbo		Trinidad Kalenda
Scotch Igbo		
Temné		
Moko Yégéyégé		
Moko Bange		
Added dances		
Scotch Chamba	Quelbe (Boula)	[Woman Kalenda]
Scotch Kongo	Bongo Sorti	
	Dama	

Sources: Pearse 1956; Pearse 1978–79.

The Big Drum is usually more ritualistically mounted with food offerings and essential symbols in place at the insistence of an ancestor who appears in a "dream message" or from a personally timed cycle triggered by the knowledge that a social display of goodwill and a return of thanks for success must be offered. It may also be convened at a critical time when the support of the spirit world must be assured—usually at the reconstruction of the family or the transformation of its status within the society. In the same way that a marriage, a newly built house, or the acquisition of a boat alters the status of the family, so also is the family affected by death and often ceremonializes the anniversary of a death as well as the other adjustments to family structure by hosting a dance. Any Carriacou family may host a Big Drum.

Family Big Drum celebrations are open to the community, and large boat launchings attract what appears to be the entire island. Before I became familiar with the policy, I asked a young person if he were invited to a particular dance. He explained to me with humor that he would, of course, go: "They didn't tell me not to come!"

The family mounts the feast in the "yard," the modest grounds surrounding the house, the private place into which only friends enter. Within African belief systems of the Caribbean, the yard is considered a spiritual space in terms of its situational and emotional linkages (Mintz 1974:246). Within this arena the wake and the four successive funeral observances (the third night, the "nine night," the fortieth night, and the stone feast) take place. For many years after the head stone has been erected at the stone feast, sacrifices and libations unifying the lineage and commemorating the deceased may take place on that family ground (McDaniel 1985).

Ceremony Outline

To assure the success of its Big Drum, the host family prepares carefully. A tarpaulin may be erected in case of rain, lamps are readied, benches are borrowed, and cases of beer and bottles of rum are ordered. The men finish butchering the animals early in the morning so that ritual foods get the assigned attention from the women in the community, who seem to gather without being summoned, some toting utensils just in case the host does not own a large enough pot. They commence their service without instruction, stirring the traditional corn staple coucou in a huge pot or molding individual portions of "roll rice." The largest portions of the mutton, pork, and chicken are steamed over outdoor fires, but a select batch of this food is set aside to be prepared without salt for the ancestors.

Pearse noted the structure of the Big Drum practiced during the 1950s in this way: 1: Warm-up; 2: Opening Ring; 3: Evocation and Free Ring; 4: Cromanti, Igbo, and Manding songs; 5: Beg Pardon; 6: Cut Neck; 7: Parents' Plate; 8: Farewell to Ancestors; 9: Dawn-Dance-Ending songs (Pearse n.d.). The ritual concert takes place within a circle formed by a standing crowd, three male drummers, and a group of from five to twelve female singer/dancers. The singers and drummers are led by the female leader, the chantwell. The Patois word *chantwell* (often spelled *chantuelle* or, for the male leader, *chanterel*) has fallen from use, but in the early decades of this century it was in wide usage throughout the Francophone and Franglophone Caribbean. The word also refers to a caged bird used to attract other birds (Robert 1984:286). The French origin of the word is *chanterelle*, denoting the highest string on an instrument. On the hurdy-gurdy the chanterelle differentiates the "singing" stop from the complementary drone of the other stops (Sadie 1980:148).

As song leader, the chantwell teaches the repertoire, introduces the songs, and spurs on the drummers and singers at the performance. She uses a chac-chac, a maraca constructed from a boli-gourd, to steady and control rhythms and to create a sheet of sound behind the drum rhythms.

According to firmly established rules, three drums (a cutter and two boulas) accompany the chantwell and chorus. The boulas respond to the vocal introduction of each song by announcing the specific beat of the song. After the boulas' entry, the cutter follows with dramatic, asymmetrical improvisational lines that introduce the dancer, who, like the last voice in a fugal exposition, enters the ring. Each song reflects this entry pattern.

The dance ritual commences with two or three shortened performances of Creole songs as a warm-up. After this staid prelude the first dance must be appropriate to the ethnic origins of the host—and here the revelry begins. The oldest male of the host family, with guests remarking and laughing, leads a dancing procession of family members into the dance ring. As head of the house, he pours rum on the earth, his wife sprinkles water, and others in the line scatter corn and rice as ancestral offerings. After the entrance of the family, the host dances with a towel in each hand. Finally he places the towels in a crossed position on the ground, marking the cardinal points or pathways, preparing an entry for the visiting ancestors. Whoops of laughter accompany this segment, especially when "old heads" attempt to "wind" convincingly with stiffened hips or to turn securely on worn-out and swollen feet. Each family member takes her or his turn dancing with the towels until the final dancer in the family procession places them on the drum head as a signal of closure (Procope 1955:126).

In the first of the three Cromanti songs that signal the beginning of the main segment of the ritual, the "old hoe," or any metal object, is struck by a spoon. The timbre and musical function of this idiophone are analogous to that of the African bell-gong. Its symbolic call summons the ancestors and announces the privileged time for the invited ancestors to dance. The dance ring is now reserved for them. Humans are forbidden to occupy the "free ring"; it is believed that misfortune attacks those who unknowingly enter its center. At this introduction, the ancestors are called to be fed, entertained, and—with this "attention"—remembered. "What better way to remember the ancestors," declare culture bearers, "than having to feed them!"

Though no longer often the practice, if the feast were celebrated at a new yard, the entire ensemble and guests would walk to the parents' former house during the proceedings to commemorate the ancestral site. The natural break would take place before midnight, when ritual food and rum would be distributed. After the meal, to commence the second part of the ceremony, the more deeply evocative Midnight Cromanti and Midnight Manding would be heard. These were accompanied by the old hoe or a bell gong sound of a spoon on a bottle that is reserved for communicating with the spirit world. Again, after the ancestral calling, the more lively singing of the huge repertoire would resume and the dancing would continue until daybreak. During this time many people were enticed into dancing their national rhythms or favorite songs, which were sometimes reserved for them alone.

Today the sequence outlined above is revised to a shortened program accompanied by less elaborate food preparations. However, the pleasure of the dance persists and the crowd always seems to observe the dancing intently, responding to a beautiful execution with a unified "ohhhhh," or with laughter when an old man unsteadied by rum tries to mimic the movements of the dancers. The guests always scream with delight at the sensuous winding of the Chiffoné dance and openly critique the performance: "She too young to be so rude!" At the evening's end a song that seems to fall outside of the general repertoire, "All Over," is chanted. Also called the Powder dance, it accompanies the playful dousing of the guests with talcum powder.

The lightheartedness of the guests signals the memorial's acceptance by the ancestors and indicates their pleasure at the human attention bestowed upon them. If the energy of the dance is deemed low, it was perhaps due to the omission of a specific element in the ritual order. In such a case the entire play would have to be restaged.

Each of the symbolic events outlined above infuses the program with reason from the past; even the sequence of songs bears meaning. I suggest that during a specific era in the evolution of the ritual, song order indicated social privilege and ethnic dominance of one group over another. The crucial program structure consists of three Cromanti, three Igbo, and three Manding songs. I hypothesize that the social structure, mirrored by the structure of items in the Big Drum musical program, was ruled by a three-nation congress—the Cromanti, the Igbo, and the Manding. A colonial census document ("State of the Island," 1775) in part supports my music-based conjecture on Cromanti dominance. It reveals the plurality of both the Cromanti and Igbo by providing a column to indicate the number of runaways "of which Cormantees" and "of which Ebboes." No other nation is mentioned on the census. Besides their numerical advantage, other bases by which the Cromanti would have dominated the Nation dance will be discussed later.

During the early decades of this century, men participated more frequently in the dance than they do today, but despite the male presence the event was even then known to have been controlled by mature women. Two chantwells now active in the dance are Lucian Duncan of Mount Royal village and Estimie Andrews of Harvey Vale village. Duncan's group comprises older dancers, and Andrews, in collaboration with Christine David, passes the repertoire on to the younger women of the Carriacou Cultural Organization (CCO). That organization was formed more than fifteen years ago as a "duty inspired by memory" to keep the dance tradition alive. The young women and girls recruited to the CCO years ago are now mature dancers.

Estimie Andrews's reminiscence of her grandmother's participation in the Big Drum around 1937 affords insight into the generational bonding, the behavior of participants, and the mood during the late night intermission in the ritual.

I always followed MaTai to the Big Drum. I would carry and guard the straw bag that always accompanied her. It contained her pipe, a towel and an empty bottle. During the intermission when the musicians are fed, I would go by the fireside and catch my grandmother's pipe with a fire stick and hand it to her. Instead of drinking the strong Jack Iron rum offered, MaTai instructed me to put her portion into our empty bottle to be stored at home. When the dancing began again I would fall asleep.

The most meaningful and spiritual song/dances were performed at the resumption of the dance, when the child (Estimie) would be fast asleep. The songs performed late at night belong to the Midnight Cromanti type and are classified as Beg Pardon songs. Participants petitioning the ancestors danced on their knees singing "Mene mwê conté" (Help me to declare). Andrew Pearse mentions the mordant Coupé Cou ("cru-cru" or "cut neck"), a minor ritual and healing dance, that was also performed after midnight. The mock stickfighting symbolized the character of the spiritual defenses against the forces of evil while the wiping and brushing motions made by a kneeling dancer around her neck symbolized the taking of an oath (the cutting of the neck).

Besides the loss of the inscrutable Coupé Cou ritual, the contemporary ritual has lost, since the 1950s, about eighty songs. Pearse lists a corpus of two hundred songs, and since my initial research in 1983 I have gathered 129 songs and song fragments in use or in the memory of old heads (see song list in appendix 1). The ceremony is also now reduced in length, seldom continuing past midnight. Carriacouans perceive the diminishment in several aspects but most often speak of the loss of male dance partners. The absence of male dancers is especially felt in the Bélè Kawé where a man escorts two female dancers into the ring.

Since my involvement the major loss in the Big Drum has been the death of the old head drummers who were specialists, not only in drumming styles, but also in the song literature and in ceremonial principles.

Dance Description

Dancers perform singly in the Nation dances, and in the Cromanti, Igbo, and Manding dances they assume a bent contour. The body and knees bend at an angle to the earth at varying degrees, with the intrepid Manding dance exhibiting the lowest crouch. The low posture and crooked knees integrate the initial dances, and the idiosyncratic symbolic hand gesture in each individualizes them. Dance variations include the open palms of penitence (as in the Cromanti and Igbo), the physical trembling that might accompany exorcism portrayed long ago in the Chamba and Arada dances (David 1979:21), and dancing on knees (as in the Midnight Cromanti and Coupé Cou).

The distinguishing elements of the Creole dances include an uplifted stance, the extension of the winged skirt, and partner dancing. The Frivolous dances, conforming to the sexual innuendoes of the texts, exploit aggressive, winding hip movements. The facial expression, stony and dispassionate, remains fixed upon the partner's hips while the crowd exhibits wild approval with roars of laughter and goading exclamations of "Give it to her!" and "Ai, dancer!"

In solo dances the dancer faces the three drummers, and the eyes of the center drummer focus on her feet. Her foot movements dictate the lead drummer's improvisation mode, for he converts the movement of her steps into audible rhythmic patterns.

After the soloist completes her exhibition, she exchanges positions with another dancer by rotating with the second dancer in the "wheel," each holding the other about the waist with one arm, first swinging counterclockwise then clockwise. At this the drummer "breaks," changing from sporadic rhythms to even metric pulses, resuming the highly syncopated pattern when the new dancer is ready. The wheel, in which dancers are introduced and exit and which appears in all dance types, appears European and strangely incongruous with the movement and style of the Nation dances.

The dancer signals the end of the piece by touching the drumhead with the hem of her skirt, or, in the case of a male dancer, with his towel. Here the interaction between drummer and dancer as portrayed by the husband-and-wife team Sugar Adams and May Fortune is fondly described by Carriacou teacher Roy Benjamin:

> There was something unspoken between them. Once May got into the ring and Sugar started to drum, there would be some message passing between them and all of a sudden you'd find yourself . . . you'd be infected with it. You just started to notice the dance much more closely. . . . Once she started dancing and really getting . . . she

MR. CANUTE. CALISTE GARRIG
CAR

4. "The Big Drum,"
by Canute Caliste.

would dance as though for him and he would play for her as though this was something just for each other. People were here, yes, but the dance was as though something sacred between them.

The reminiscences of culture bearers help re-create an earlier style of Big Drum apparel, when dancers wore the "open" skirt, modeled in the French colonial fashion, called the *douette* (douiette). The lavish and colorful douette skirt was made with a train that sometimes incorporated eight yards of material (Macdonald 1962:48) and was split in the front to expose a luxuriant white, starched petticoat made from bleached flour-bag material with ribbon woven through the embroidered hemline. The hem of one side of the outer skirt was stylishly tucked into the waistband, or sometimes removed and held if the dance mode warranted it, one hem edge in each hand. Dancing barefoot, the women's dress included the African head-tie, earrings, and the colonial gown. The douette style continues today in a simplified form, but the older folk say that the younger dancers do not wear the "proper" embroidered underwear under the current, more modestly and simply constructed outer skirt.

While drummers may don dashikis, the male dancer does not generally wear a costume. However, he uses towels in each hand to "shape the dance." Men who dance are usually either drummers who relinquish their musical positions to take a turn in the ring or spectators who, inspired by the boula drum cadence of the nation, simply jump into the ring (Corion 1983).

Carriacou History and People

Carriacou is governed by Grenada; its political history is Grenada's, and Grenada's colonial tussles and rebellions are also Carriacou's. One of the earliest contests over Grenada's verdant, lush land, described as "prime real estate" by then U.S. secretary of state George Shultz (*New York Times*, Feb. 8, 1984:A3), occurred between France and England in the seventeenth century. Both countries simultaneously claimed Grenada and Carriacou. The issue was settled for a time by France's DuParquet, who, along with two hundred "adventurers," purchased Grenada in 1650 from their host Carib chief, "and the price which was paid, was a few hatchets, a large quantity of glass beads, knives, and two bottles of brandy!!!" (*Grenada Almanac*, 1829).

5. A Big Drum audience.

But armed conflicts arose over the conditions of the agreement and, as almost every history of Grenada declares in telling the tale of the historic French/Carib battle of 1650: The French made a final pursuit of the Carib forces to a precipice from which the Caribs leapt into the sea rather than be taken hostage. The battle is memorialized in the name of the adjacent village, Sauteurs ("The Leapers") (Steele 1974:9). I include the tale not only because it resembles the plight of many enslaved Africans, but also because it is emblematic of the long history of rebellion in Grenada.

The faces of the present population reveal no Carib inheritance; except for a few survivors, the Carib nation has been annihilated on Grenada and Carriacou. Despite this, Carib history on Carriacou is unequivocal and evidenced by the wide range of pottery fragments appearing daily on the shorelands. The abundance of earth-tone Amerindian archeological artifacts testifies to the former ownership of the land and the active material culture of the early inhabitants. During the 1988 erection of the Harvey Vale beachfront guesthouse, Constant Spring, workmen digging to accommodate a concrete pillar for the raised structure struck a well. The flowing fresh water was found to be contained by large earthen pots without bottoms, embedded within one another to form the cylinder of the well. Identified as Carib pots, they are now housed in the Carriacou Historical Museum.

Like the well, and like shards that suddenly appear in freshly hoed gardens, a few words of Amerindian origin emerge in Carriacouan speech: any simple wooden structure may be called by the Carib name *ajoupa*, which originally meant a rustic thatched dwelling. The word *titere*, meaning a small edible fish, is often thought to be of Carib origin. It is incorporated in the Big Drum song "Titere Surrender" in which children are referred to as little fish. Mabouya, an uninhabited island near Carriacou, gets its name from the Carib word meaning "evil spirit" (Hughes 1966:48). And finally, the name *Carriacou*, spelled *Karyouacou*, *Cariouwacou* (Kay 1971:8), or *Kayryouacou* in seventeenth- and eighteenth-century writings and maps, is most likely of Carib origin.

Like Grenada, Carriacou was a French colony for only 117 years (1650–1763 and 1779–83), but despite the relatively short period and the remoteness in time, aspects of French culture persist other than the language survivals in the Big Drum. Erected on the major British-named lookout points on Carriacou—Gun Point, Pegus Point, and Belair—are ancient cannons that appear to protect the Franco-named villages of L'ance la Roche, Beausejour, La Resourse, Bay a L'eau, Petit Carenage, and Mt. D'or. The cannons also oversee the smaller Patois-named districts La Kai ("The House") and Pi Salé ("Salt Well"). The family names or "titles" Bedeau, Caliste, Noel, Baptiste, Romaine, and Mundi reflect the French colonial past, while names like Adams, Duncan, St. John, David, McClaren, Lawrence, and McDonald recall the English and Scottish presence. Village names sometimes reveal mixed national identities as well as disconcerting phonological parallels. One example of this is the name of the village of Ti Bo (Ti Beau or T'Igbo), which some people assume gets its name from the Igbo gravesite in that village. However, according to maps the village site was named after the Thibault estate (Brinkley 1987).

The French revolutionary spirit had a dramatic effect in the West Indies, especially on the Francophone islands. Rebellions were common in the late eighteenth century. The growing number of Africans was felt to be dangerous, and every effort was taken by the colonial government to dismantle and suppress African dances. The legal code of 1808, inscribed in *The Laws of Grenada from 1763 to 1805*, made the ban on drumming and therefore dancing very clear:

> That whatsoever Master . . . shall suffer any slaves to beat any Drum . . . or empty Casks or Boxes or great Gourds, or to blow Horns, Shells

or loud Instruments, for the Diversion or Entertainment of Slaves,
. . . who do not suppress the same in one Hour after the same begins
. . . shall be convicted; . . . (G. Smith 1808:10)

In his ethnography of Carriacou, Donald Hill includes a 1798 quote from the *St. George's Chronicle and Grenada Gazette* that suggests that the dance event was a place of meeting for enslaved people and incendiary "disorderly free people of colour" (1977:314). Slave proprietors saw the drum as a disruptive force associated with rebellion and therefore sought to replace it with "a fiddle or two," thinking that the violin would in time become "more pleasing" than the drum.[1]

Despite attempts to control the enslaved population, rebellions overwhelmed Haiti, Guadeloupe, Martinique, Dominica, and St. Lucia. In Grenada in 1795, Julien Fedon, the propertied son of an African mother and a French planter father, led an army of free and enslaved Africans and "free coloureds," fighting under the French flag, held the British army at bay for a year and a half. The Fedon Rebellion, unleashed on March 2, 1795, is significant to many Grenadians as a symbol of the people's power (Sunshine 1982:19). Any actual involvement of Carriacouans in that struggle cannot be determined from the Grenadian handbook, which reads:

> It is pleasant to note . . . that the slaves in Carriacou were faithful and well behaved during the rebellion, and this, too, although there was no garrison there, and they outnumbered their masters by at least forty to one. (Extracts from the Grenada Handbook, CQ, 1974:65)

In actuality, however, a Carriacouan, Joachim Philip, served under Julien Fedon as one of his most trusted captains. Philip was a cotton planter born into a wealthy mixed-race family. The family owned the entire island of Petit Martinique to the north of Carriacou along with several properties on Grenada and Carriacou. It is not known if Joachim Philip was among the many mixed-race leaders of the rebellion who were finally arrested and executed (McDaniel 1990). Similarly, the fate of Fedon himself remains a mystery—in the lore of the people he is believed to have "flown" away to safety.

Ten years after the Fedon Rebellion, colonists grew alarmed that a plot to murder whites was underway. The leaders of the conspiracy were in communication with a group from Bequia, an island in the Windward Islands near St. Vincent that had recently experienced a revolt. The following letter includes a request for protection during this period of unrest.

To Same Wyndham

Sir,
On the second of the month two gentlemen proprietors from the island of Carriacou, Mr. Wm. Scott and G. McLean, came to me with a representation that the inhabitants of that island were alarmed from some appearance among their slaves that they thought dictated a mutinous disposition and they reported that an attempt had taken place in Bequia, a neighboring island in the government of St. Vincent, which had been discovered and the ring leaders taken and sent to St. Vincent for trial, that the instigators were leaders in Carriacou, were in close correspondence by canoes with the Bequia negros, and that their intentions were to murder all the white people and seize the small craft in which they were to escape to Santo Domingo. Beckwith, who confirmed the account as far as it respects Bequia and the two negros had been found guilty but the plot having discovered before much progress had been made the evidence would not enable them to convict others. *An insurrection in such a place or places was never thought of before and the negros of Carriacou were uncommonly faithful and well behaved during the revolt in Grenada of 1795–6.* (Brinkley n.d.; emphasis added)

Despite the praise Carriacouans received for docility, the smaller and even individual revolts that often occurred suggest a very different disposition. There were repeated newspaper accounts of physical escape that should be regarded as stories of personal rebellion. Two of these are significant "run-away" accounts from 1790 and 1798, published in Grenada's *St. George's Chronicle*, describing the flight of five enslaved men from Carriacou. The articles include a thorough description of each man's physique, clothing, trade, language, and *nation* (among the group were men from the Kongo and Igbo nations). The word *Creole* in the descriptions meant simply that the runaways were not from Africa but the Caribbean.[2]

On the night of Tuesday the 17th current, ran away from the island of Carriacou, in a small fishing canoe, two Negroes, one named Jack, a house servant, of the Conga [*sic*] nation. Speaks both French and English; formerly the property of Mr. Patrick Kewley, and well-known in the town of St. Georges. About 5 feet five inches high; had on when he went away a check shirt an Oznaburgh breeches a brown cloth coat with red cape and cuff.

The other named Jame, by trade a carpenter, of the Ibo nation, a yellow complexion, and aged about 26 years, wore an Oznaburgh frock and trowsers; he was lately bought of Mr. William Johnstone, and is also well known in St. George's, it is supposed that they must have landed on some part of Grenada, as the canoe was too small to carry them to the main. Any person apprehending the above Negroes. . . . (*St. George's Chronicle and New Grenada Gazette*, Aug. 19, 1790)

Runaway this day from this island in a canoe, three negro men in the property of Peter Pegus, viz. Jean Francoise from the Heritage Estate, a creole, about 20 years of age, stout made, of a very black complexion, and a good deal pock pitted, about 5 feet 6 inches high. Sylvester from the same Estate, a young creole, about 18 years of age, well made, and of brownish complexion, about 5 feet 8 inches high.

Janga, from Union Estate, a young creole, about 22 years of age, well made, and of a very black complexion, about five feet 8 inches high. N.B. They all speak French and English, and as it is supposed they are landed in Grenada, a reward of 5 Joes is hereby offered. (*St. George's Chronicle and Grenada Gazette*, Sept. 14, 1798)

The modern history of Carriacou began with clashes between the French and the original Amerindian inhabitants, and repercussions of these conflicts echo in the later battles between French and English settlers. Upon this hostile canvas other patterns of aggression and flight are etched, by enslaved Africans as well as Amerindians in the later period of slavery.

Given the size of the island, the population of 6,000 should be considered undersized. In 1750 the population consisted of only 202 "souls"—or in the census as corrected by Brinkley, 199 souls (Brinkley 1978:53). This extraordinary census lists every member of the leading families, by name and often with a description. Later census listings simply note race and whether a person was enslaved or free. In 1773 there were 2,700 blacks and 100 whites living on Carriacou; in 1778 there were 3,046 enslaved persons and 107 whites and "a number of "Free Mulattoes and Negroes" ("Description of the Grenadines," 1778).

In 1829 there were 3,452 enslaved persons, 45 whites, and 303 "coloreds" (*Grenada Almanac*, 1829:130); in 1833 there were 3,200 enslaved and 800 free people (*Bristol Mirror*, June 15, 1833; cited in Smith 1962a:22). We can see the effect of the 1763 British takeover in the population surge reported in 1773. The lack of growth between the years 1778 and 1829 reflects the loss of lives as the outcome of the Fedon Rebellion, which fractured Grenada, forcing the revolutionaries and the French to take refuge in Trinidad.

The Bongo songs that I turn to first elucidate the system that patterned the physical displacement of the runagate African prisoners. They tell of the separation and dispersal of families and recount the pain and longing for home that influenced their flights of desertion.

Though no longer included in contemporary programming, these Bongo songs are familiar to Big Drum practitioners. A legendary incident must have generated this first lament, a multi-stanza item mourning the children Zabette and Walter's loss of their parents, who had been sold and shipped individually to Haiti and Trinidad or perhaps to Antigua. The following text was gathered by Pearse, who notes that "Hele is . . . bawling, that is wailing noisily—and sometimes merely conventionally—at funerals" (Pearse 1956:4). The voice in the song is that of the parents.

Pléwé Mwê Lidé [Bongo]

Pléwé mwê Lidé, Pléwé Maiwaz, oh
Hélé mwê, Lidé, hélé oh, Maiwaz
Hélé pu nu alé

Dimâsh pwoshî bâtma-la-vol-a Haishi
Vâdi ya bâtmâ-la-vol-a kité, oh, Maiwaz

Sa ki kôtâ mwê, kôsolé yish mwê ba mwê
Sa ki kôtâ mwê, kôsolé Zabette ba mwê
Sa ki émê mwê, kôsolé Walter ba mwê. (Pearse 1956:4)

Weep for Me

Weep for me, Lydia, weep, Mary Rose
Lament for me, Lydia, lament Mary Rose
Lament for us all

Sunday next, the schooner sails for Haiti
Friday the schooner leaves Haiti

Whoever loves me, console my children for me
Whoever loves me, console Zabette for me
Whoever loves me, console Walter for me.

The names in this song are significant, and I suggest that they appear not only as an inherited characteristic from parent musics but for reasons of history keeping. Each song incorporates a name, either of an ancestor, the subject of the song, the song composer, or, in the oldest songs, places such as Dahomey, Arada, Kongo, or Haiti.

Names are known to be a central cultural marker among the Asanti and, in this study, they have been useful to my research on lineages and personal histories. It is not surprising that the names in the song above (except Lidé) and several other song names (Ovid, Antoine, Derrick, Roselia) appear in the 1842–49 Anglican Register.

A second text, consonant in theme with "Pléwé mwê Lidé," may have been an offshoot of it, for not only do the names *Lidé* and *Maiwaz* appear in this song of consolation, but the dance type is again a Bongo.

Maiwaz-o [Bongo]

Maiwaz-o-o-a, ai, ai
Maiwaz-o, ai, Lidé-a-e
Maiwaz-o, ai, Mama
Vini ouè mwê
Maiwaz, mokai windé plewé

Ba kai palé
Maiwaz, mokai windé kosé
Maiwaz-o, ai, Mama
Vini ouè mwê

Mary Rose-o

Mary Rose-o, ai
Mary Rose-o, ai, Lydia

Mary Rose-o, ai, Mama
Come see me
Mary Rose, I will help you cry

I will not speak
Mary Rose, I will help you babble
Mary Rose-o, Mama
Come see me

The Concept of Nation

In written documents of the eighteenth century the evasive term *nation* appears frequently. The word, essential to the ideal of the Big Drum, also appears in the oral literature and vernacular of Carriacouans to this day. Operating within two systems, basically, *nation* denotes not only a geographic region but a linguistic/ethnic group as well. I explore first the usage shared by the colonial class and then that of the Africans pressed into their service.

Owners of enslaved people often categorized their imprisoned servants by nation in order to manage them in reference to the cultural behaviors ascribed to each group. However, the means employed to achieve the universal goal of work productivity varied from place to place. Marie-Josée Cérol's work on the genesis of Creole languages suggests that the practice of dispersing linguistic communities because whites feared communication among Africans may not have been universal (Cérol 1992:61). On French islands, for example, homogeneous language groups were assembled. The evidence of nation gatherings on Carriacou supports her research. Cérol's hypothesis calls for more study of this practice and its effects on slave society and language.

The Cromanti nation, the historically dominant group of the Big Drum, was made up of an assemblage of Gold Coast peoples, principally Akan, who spoke Twi, Fante (a variation of Twi), and Akuapim. The Cromanti (Coromantee, Cormantine, Koromantyn, or variations of those spellings) acquired their national title from the Dutch castle-fort Cormantine, which served as their port of departure from Africa.

In like manner, an equally active Asanti port, Elmina, situated 20 miles from Cormantine, gave its name to the "Mine" slaves processed there by the Portuguese during the sixteenth century. The Mine people were also Akan and probably comprised the same peoples that were collectively called Cromanti by the British.

In the eighteenth century, terminologies employed for African nationalities were vague and indiscriminate, and the Portuguese, Dutch, English, and French used separate terms. Often the geographic port of exit, the regional city annexed to the port, or the language/culture of the group was chosen as national title (Curtin 1969:189). Of the Carriacou nations, the Igbo and Temne retained their ethnic denomination, while Manding referred to peoples principally from Senegal and Gambia, as well as those from several linguistic areas between Cape Roxo to Cape Appollonia (Edwards 1793:50). They were called Mandingue by the French and Mandingo by the English (Curtin 1969:185). The Arada (or Rada) took their national denomination from the powerful Dahomean culture/kingdom centered in the city Ardrah, which appears as Allada on late-eighteenth-century maps.

The Moko group was assumed by Edwards (1794:52) to be related to the Igbo, but living further north in the interior. Fyfe (1963:170) proposes that they were from the area of the Cameroon, and Crow (1830:299) calls them Quaws. With this information we may conjecture that the Moko were Ibibios. However, Curtin suggests that they were "a diverse range of peoples and cultures shipped from slave ports on the lower Cross River" of the Bight of Biafra. He also states that the Kongo peoples were an even broader range of Bantu-speaking groups from western Central Africa. The Chamba (or Thiamba) were taken from the Bight of Benin (Curtin 1969:188). Pinpointing the area from which the Banda were taken presents a peculiar problem: several Banda groups could conceivably have been raided for the capture of people. I propose that the Banda may either be the group from the Gold Coast interior that experienced Asanti invasion around 1765 (Wilks 1975:246n.21) or the Banda nation from Central Africa. I use the Banda song texts that include Akan names to weigh the selection in favor of the Banda from the Gold Coast, but other factors challenge that conclusion, and the matter is not yet settled.

Table 2 lists the colonial regions in Africa from which the early generations of Carriacou people were kidnapped. Figure 6 is a map of present-day ethnic nations.

Table 2. Regions in colonial Africa from which Carriacouans originated

Nation	Region	Modern nations
Cromanti	Gold Coast	Ghana
Igbo	Bight of Biafra	Nigeria (southeastern)
Manding	Senegambia, Mali	Senegambia, Mali
Temne	Sierra Leone	Sierra Leone, Liberia
Kongo	Congo, Central Africa	Democratic Republic of the Congo
Chamba	Bight of Biafra	Nigeria
Moko	Bight of Biafra	Nigeria, Cameroon
Banda	Gold Coast interior or Central Africa	Ghana or Congo

The following excerpt from a British description of the Gold Coast fort Cormantine was written in 1812. Figure 7 presents three contemporary views of the fort in its restored state.

About three miles from Annamaboe is situated the town of Coromantine, where the Dutch have a fort, called Amsterdam. It was built by the English, and was the first fort erected by us on the Gold-Coast. It is on an eminence that overlooks the sea, which renders it particularly airy. It was taken in 1662, or 1663, by the Dutch admiral De Ruyter; since which period it has continued to be possessed by that nation. . . . It has been observed, that the Ashantees, in 1807, found their way into this fort, and plundered it of what provisions it contained; since which, the place has been neglected. The Fantees residing in Annamaboe, advantage of this neglect, demanded of the Dutch government the sum of forty ounces, under threat of destroying the fort, . . . The Dutch government would not comply . . . the Annamaboes marched out, headed by their king; . . . [the fort] was pillaged; the guns rendered useless, part of walls levelled, and the artificers attached to it made prisoners. [Annamaboe] and Cormantine . . . were the greatest markets for slaves on the Gold-Coast: it was not uncommon to see from twenty to thirty sail of shipping, of different nations, trading here together. (Meredith 1812:130).

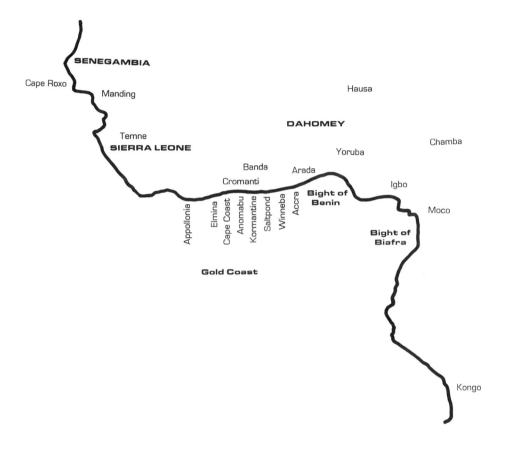

6. West Coast and Gold Coast of Africa

7. Three contemporary views of Fort Cormantine.

In spite of this chronicle verifying "Coromantine" as one of the largest and earliest English slave ports on the Gold Coast, no mention of enslaved Akan or Cromanti people appears in the French Carriacou census of 1750. Colonial powers were evidently limited to nations housed and transported from their own forts on West Africa. Among those identified by nation in the French-owned enslaved population that numbered 202 "souls" were:

8 Congo
3 Arrada [Arada]
3 Bambara
1 Moque [Moko]
1 Mondong [possibly Moundong or Monding (Manding)]
2 Igbo
3 Aura [possibly Aro, an Igbo subgroup]
1 Anan [or Anang, Western Ibibio] (Brinkley 1978:54)

Because Cromanti people were brought to Carriacou soon after 1763, when the island was ceded to the British, "Cormantees and Ebboes" (Igbos) appear prominently in the 1775 British census. By that time, however, Cormantine had been taken by the Dutch, and therefore people enslaved by the British did not exit from there. Nevertheless, West Indian planters continued to call their Gold Coast captives Cromanti (van Dantzig 1980:23), a name that bore meaning to them.

Cromanti dominance is curiously documented in colonial writings that characterize them as excelling other nations in music (Abrahams 1983:293) and as possessing "a ferociousness of disposition; but withal courage and a stubbornness or what an ancient Roman would have deemed an elevation of soul" (Edwards 1793:63).

I speculate that soon after their arrival the Cromanti came to dominate the nine-nation slave society, not only in musico-ritual domains but in other activities by virtue of their numbers and forceful presence.

The songs themselves may help to refine the data offered above with evidence from an internal voice coming from a new perspective. Songs serve, states Ghanaian musicologist Kwabena Nketia,

as depositories of information on African societies and their way of life, as records of their histories, beliefs, and values. In some African societies, deliberate attempts are made to use songs for educating the young—at initiation camps, for example—or for transmitting information. Instances can be found of the formal use of song for making announcements or proclamations, expressing gratitude or appreciation to a benefactor, serenading lady loves, warning, advising, or boasting. Sometimes what cannot be said in speech can be stated in song. (1974:204)

The Musical Interpretation

Henry Louis Gates outlines the interpretive processes of reassembling, reifying, and merging disparate texts by which I arrive at conclusions in this study.

> Because of the experience of diaspora, the fragments that contain the traces of a coherent system of order must be reassembled. These fragments embody aspects of a theory of critical principles around which the discrete texts of the tradition configure, in the critic's reading of the textual past. To reassemble fragments, of course, is to engage in an act of speculation, to attempt to weave a fiction of origins and subgeneration. It is to render the implicit as explicit, and at times to imagine the whole from the part. (1988:xxiv)

Gates proposes a special quality in the "experience of diaspora" and suggests that this aspect demands a special scholarship. The African experience in the "new world" confounded history keeping to such an extent that "no stories from the Middle Passage survive" (Morrison 1987). The notion of a specialized scholarship that reassembles or weaves fragments, or that "render[s] the implicit as explicit," is fairly radical in its thrust to expand the sparse clues to display a historical culture fully. The terms "fiction," "speculation," and "imagination" as used by Gates are usually considered distinct and mutually exclusive of the methods employed by researchers writing history. However, because this work searches history as perceived by the "old parents" and exposed through their songs, there must be a reclaiming of a certain subjectivity here. Just as the myth of the flying Africans carries several layers of truth, its interpretation influences my speculation on the imagination of the people's creation of a "coherent system of order."

A specific musical aesthetic undergirds the ancient texts; a music that serves as the banister upon which the poetic systems lean and survive. The musical meanings are also based on conjecture, as the multiplex gloss of the texts will show, but to strengthen my interpretation in the search for musical etymologies, I will list, either in the text or in the notes, the several alternatives in the musico/linguistic puzzles that follow.

The Concept of Nation in Song

The concept of nation as held by the people is a difficult one to explicate, for its dimensions include social, spiritual, living, and ancestral systems of kinship. These varied expressions of the nation ideal emerged and exhibited themselves within many ritual types formed by slave societies in the Americas.

In the next section of this work nation texts are scrutinized and the origins of the African-sounding words and names are fished out of the vast pool of language sources. Early on I found that the ritual texts, though neatly organized by nation, are filled with unlikely borrowings that were evidence of widely diffused and protracted historical culture contacts. Many choices for etymological connections were offered me; in fact, besides the nine African-language choices, Carib, English, French, English Patois, and French Patois sources are all congruent with the history of the Cromanti. Even the Yoruba and Hausa languages should be included in this language pool, because, although they are absent from the demographic history of Carriacou, these languages are preserved in the accessible Sango rituals of Grenada and Trinidad. When migrating Carriacouans returned home from Trinidad, they influenced the Nation-song language in the same way they reorganized and accreted evolving Frivolous dance styles from neighboring islands onto the Big Drum.

As in the ritual order, Cromanti songs will be presented first, then songs from the Igbo and Manding repertoires will follow. Items from the repertoire of the other six nations follow the three-nation introductory program.

Cromanti Songs

The Cromanti song "Cromanti Cudjo" presents problems of lost meanings, text variations, and multiple interpretations. In the first example the lead singer invites Cromanti Cudjo, a venerated ancestor, and the chorus responds, "That's my nation, come."

Cromanti Cudjo [Cromanti]

C'est nation mwê sa
Webe nu
Cromanti Cudjo
C'est nation mwê sa
Webe nu

Cromanti Cudjo
That's my nation
Come!
Cromanti Cudjo
That's my nation
Come!

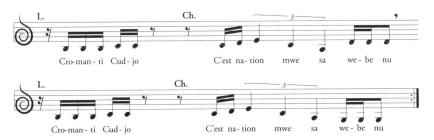

Aged people, the old heads of the community informed me that they did not know the meaning of *webe nu* (webe no), but they did offer possible origins from which the abstruse phrase could have derived: *mwê beno* ("I bless"), *weve nu* ("our dream"), or *leve nu* ("let us get up"). My procedure in searching for lost meanings in texts was as follows: I first sought a Patois origin, then a colonial or mixed-language root. If I found no cognates, I explored African roots. During this search I discovered the term *webe nu* in the autobiography of the Grenadian religious leader Norman Paul. In his life history, *Dark Puritan*, transcribed by M. G. Smith, he recalls a personal vision in which the phrase is used to summon the ancestors:

> And my mother has a bottle of rum, she was throwing; I was throwing corn and we went outside the yard and we were dancing and she was singing, calling the spirit; I know that is what they used to call the spirit. . . . She have an old hoe in her hand and she beating and she singing, she have rum throwing.

Ista webe no
Webe no webe
Ista webe no . . . (Paul 1963:82)

Webe no also appears in a variant of "Cromanti Cudjo" that belongs to the Beg Pardon genre of songs. Beg Pardon songs are employed in sacrificial contexts to supplicate the ancestor spirits. Cromanti Cudjo and Mama Nu are ancestors of the Cromanti nation and, as such, are invited to join the dance and cure the afflicted. The Midnight Cromanti songs bear the deepest spiritual significance and are sung at midnight when spirits return to the festivities. As Beg Pardons, they were in earlier times danced in kneeling position.

Cromanti Cudjo
C'est malad nu sa
webe no (D. Hill 1980:7)

Cromanti Cudjo
There is sickness here
Come!

A second Cromanti song, "Anancy-o, Sari Baba," presents equally difficult problems of text translation. Clearly, Anancy is the name of the well-known creator-god, the spider of Akan provenance of the Nancy stories, which continue among a few Carriacou narrators. But the etymology of the word *sari* is not so easily found. Big Drum practitioners, beleaguered by inquiries from outsiders on the meaning of *sari* in this, one of the most popular Big Drum songs, often respond that the word means nothing and that it is just a song word or a name.

Because a Patois or English word of similar phonetic structure could not be found, I searched for Twi or Akuapim words that sounded like "sari" or "sali." Since they were not found in Akan languages, the word must have been loaned from another national usage.

The words in question may be rooted in deeper historical contexts. On the Gold Coast and among the Asanti of Kumasi, contact with Muslims was established not only through trade but as a result of the Asanti nation's expansion to the north. Instead of executing or enslaving Muslim captives, the Asanti normally absorbed them into Kumasi culture. The captured "Ashante Moslems" grew in numbers in Kumasi during Osei Kwame's reign from 1777 to 1800 and developed a Moslem community there. It is known that the Koran was greatly respected among rulers like Osei Kwame, who was sympathetic to Islam and who had visitors from the north serve him in religious capacities, as scribes recording war casualties, and for the writing of treaties (Wilks 1961:21).

Of the several choices assembled for the etymology of *sari baba*, the most compelling are *sai'ba* (pl. *sai'baba*), a Hausa word for people who have persistent bad luck (Abraham 1962:787); the Muslim Dyula name *Osei Bamba*; and the proposal by Hausa linguist Ousseina Alidou that the word *sari* is the Hausa word *tsari*, which means "protection." In Hausa, *Tsari Babba* means "the father's protection" or "the ultimate protection."

Anancy-o [Cromanti]

Anancy-o-e
Anancy-o, Sari Baba
Anancy-o, Sari Baba
Anancy-o, Sari Baba

The Midnight Cromanti group contains an equally enigmatic song with a title, "Ena," whose reference has been lost. It may be an Akan kinship term *Ena*, the Mama Nu ("our mother") referred to in the verse. Ena may be connected to the Hausa female spirit Inna, the wife of Babba Maza, who in Hausa Bori religion rules as the mother of all spirits. Her Fulani name means "mother" (Greenberg 1966:39–40).

At first, *salamani* appeared to me to be a mixture of French and English, for *sa la* and *c'est la* may be translated "like that" or "it is." *Mani* in Creole English means "morning." This interpretation found approval from all culture bearers except Peter Benjamin, who cautioned me against a mixed-language interpretation. He believed the word to be derived from the Arabic greeting *asalama alaikun,* which means "peace be unto you." The *salla* is the Moslem daily series of prayers and *salamaini* means "middle of the night" in Hausa (Westerman 1934). Any or all of the foregoing may be the origin of *salamani.*

Ena-o [Cromanti]

Ena-o, Ena-o
Ena-o, Mama nu
Salamani-o

Ena-o, Ena-o
Ena-o, Our Mother
We greet thee

Oko is a Yoruba Goddess, a member of the Nigerian Orisa pantheon and the guardian of crops and fertility. Virtually forgotten within the transplanted Orisa ritual of Trinidad, the memory of Oko has wandered, for her domain lacked usefulness to the late-arriving Yorubas, who saw distant gods as more effective to their purposes and needs. In the "new world" the enslaved population thought it absurd to entreat the God of agriculture and fecundity who would work in the favor of the colonialists, increasing their holdings and wealth (Simpson 1962:1217). However, the Yoruba deity Oko was appropriated by those living on the drought-ridden landscape of Carriacou. Their need for a more gracious environment is apparent from the many early-nineteenth-century colonial letters, reports, and newspaper articles that refer to the lack of rain and the dependence upon Grenada for food and water. Colonial documents written after 1900 speak of erosion that attacked the continually defoli-

ated land. With this ritual absorption we see a fine example of shifting religious detail and the realistic manner in which a community assembles a cosmology according to its specific needs. The song to Oko is carried by the same
melodic frame as the last melody for Ena.

Oko [Cromanti—Beg Pardon]

Oko, Oko, Oko-ye
Oko, pardoné mwê
Oko, pardoné mwê
Oko, pardoné mwê,
Oko-o, mama-o, pardoné mwê

Oko, Oko, Oko
Oko, pardon me
Oko, pardon me
Oko, pardon me
Oko, mama, pardon me

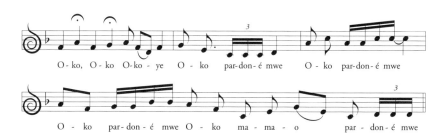

The previous texts suggest that the dance event was the essential medium
for choosing, organizing, and constructing a shared congress with new leaders
that would meet the needs of a pluralistic society. This was a society that
danced and that had already created its own language in which its communal
songs were sung. More important, we now know from the texts that the people
were dancing not only for entertainment, but were also praying to their gods
for survival, to their ancestors for pardon, healing, and deliverance. In this
way, dispossessed peoples developed personal strengths, a social organization,
and a unified congress of nine nations.

Out of the myriad cultural patterns and the shuttling of memory a new pattern of lineage was woven. The new fabric weaves in memory and sews up the broken materials from the past. However, alterations were inevitable in the reconstruction. The nations which were matrilineal in their homeland—the Cromanti and the Congo—reversed the gender base of the lineage structure in the "new world" to form a patrilineal coding. In the people's personal new worlds, accommodations of all sorts developed apart from those created by the fear and confusion in the system of slavery. French and English displaced African languages, with many people learning both languages as the plurality of runaway accounts testify. The new inclusive third language, French Creole, was assembled by the people to serve as the Lingua Franca within the freshly established Creole culture.

The geographical reality of the new population was Caribbean, but Africa persisted in memory, creating a concept of nation in which familial links remained intact despite linguistic and regional displacement. Like the duality created in the foremother in *Praisesong for the Widow*, who witnessed the reembarkation of the Igbos, the concept of nation persists in some persons, for their bodies might be in Carriacou, but their minds were "long gone with the Ibos."

Olaudah Equiano, an eighteenth-century Igbo diarist, describes his early years as a bonded person traveling through the Caribbean, Europe, North America, and to the North Pole as a ship's mate. The narrative documents his visit to Jamaica and contains his testimony on the continuity of "most of their native customs." Equiano alludes specifically to the Sunday dance ritual of about 1772 in Kingston, Jamaica, where "different nations of Africa meet and dance after the nature of their own country" (1837:128). This significant piece of information documents the concept of nation as a dance ideal of the eighteenth century, although it does not clearly indicate the formation or sequenced organization of the several dance rings, or the character of the shared program.

The valuable descriptive statement above resembles the Carriacou model in an essential way and helps to exemplify the process of ritual evolution proposed by Pearse (1978–79:638). Pearse conjectures that the several nations of early Carriacou appended their dance styles to the Cromanti ritual, creating a single, multinational Big Drum structure. The Big Drum differs from all other African-based rituals in that its program is united, but at the same time it resists complete musical and national integration.

Courlander (1960:317) suggests that the integrated Vodun complex of Haiti initially had national dances surviving intact, as presented in the Equiano description. Employing the surviving "loa" within the Vodun as clues to the original ritual makeup, Courlander states: "Had the old cults or 'nations' remained intact, the pantheons might have resembled the following: Arada or Dahomey loa, Anago or Yoruba loa, Mahi loa, Congo loa, Ibo loa, Kango loa, Petro loa, etc." I propose that multinational dances, congruent with the Courlander and Pearse theories given above, existed on Carriacou even before the British introduction of the Cromanti.

As we have seen by the narrow reporting of ethnicity in the 1750 census, among those described by nation, the Kongo group was the most evident within the early Carriacou population. Their musical and political prowess was probably overtaken by the militant Cromanti upon their later arrival into the society. The drums, central to the contemporary Big Drum, are Kongo drums, or at least called by the Kongo names *kata* (cutter) and *boula*. Thus, I speculate that the origin of the dance with Patois texts and Kongo drums may have predated the 1763 British introduction of the Cromanti. This tentative solution gives way if, as is documented on other islands, there was a late-arriving influx of Kongo people to Carriacou.

Igbo Songs

Following ritual order, the Igbo songs are presented here after the songs of the Cromanti. "Iama Diama" projects an uncompromising nationalism and also with each extemporaneous, Patois statement, "ayen ba ka fé Igbo" ("nothing can hurt the Igbo"). The word *polin* has lost precise translation, but culture bearers told me that polin is "a branch of the Igbo lineage tree." The song is often thought to contain the English phrases, "I am a" and "I ent." However, "I am a" preserves a common rhythm song word familiar to Igbo speakers, the vocable "Iyama" reported to have frequent usage in present-day Igbo ritual songs (Echewa 1985; Nzewi 1992).

The unifying lexical element in six of the seven Igbo songs is the use of *lé-lé*. The epithet "Igbo Lé-lé," also found in the Haitian Igbo pantheon, is an Igbo deity, a possessing spirit or loa also called Ianman Igbo. I hypothesize that *Iama* may share a connectedness to the Ianman Igbo loa known to Haitian Vodun participants.

Iama Diama [Igbo]

Iama diama
Igbo Lé-lé
Iama
I'm a polin Igbo
(Mwê polin Igbo)
(Ayen [I ent] ba ka fé Igbo)

Ianman, Ianman
Igbo Le-le
Ianman
I'm a polin Igbo
(I'm a polin Igbo)
(Nothing can harm the Igbo)

The following text, documented by Norman Paul as having been sung in the Grenadian Big Drum at the turn of the twentieth century, may be related to the previous Igbo song in tone and mood. Paul, recalling his grandmother, who taught him this song, explains: "She is Ibo family and she won't live for the other nations, she will trample them—that's 'Ba kakite Ibo'" (Paul 1963:7).

E-o, Ibo, Lélé-lélé
Ba ya mamma ka-ki-ti
Ba yo

Ba ya mamma sa fa me
Ibo

The sense of intolerance found in the Grenadian song above is found in a similar song, "Igbo Mauvais Nation." Neither are a part of the current Carriacou repertoire. "Igbo Mauvais Nation" was sung for me by a single culture bearer, "Petet" Frazier, a Grenadian resident formerly of Carriacou. The song exudes negative feelings toward the Igbo group and contrasts with the mood of all Carriacou Nation songs. The Carriacou Nation repertoire expresses a unified position and a positive perception of self still held by the oldest generation of Carriacou. This is clearly expressed by the Igbo drummer Sugar Adams who explains himself as part of an "African nation, a strong nation—they can fly."

Igbo Mauvais Nation [Igbo]

Igbo Lélé, Igbo Lélé
Oh, Igbo Lélé Lélé, Dahomé
Igbo mauvais nation, Dahomé
Mwê ba famil Igbo Dahomé

Igbo Lélé, Igbo Lélé
Oh, Igbo Lélé Lélé, Dahomey
Igbo is a bad nation, Dahomey
I am not of that nation, Dahomey

The next song, "Ovid-o Bagadé," describes Ovid, a distraught farmer who believes his crop to have been destroyed by a jealous neighbor who, with his eyes, laid evil energies upon his garden. Ovid's tanya plants wilt and transform into useless bushes. The community responds to his fears and confusion with support: "Ovid, don't look back, don't be afraid."

The mental control exerted against Ovid is called "maljo." The word stems from the French *mal yeux*—"evil eye." In spite of the efforts toward unification in the new society, there were personal enmities among the enslaved that reveal themselves in other song types. Conflicts of this type were brought to the dance ring, where they could be resolved within the spiritual space.

Ovid-o Bagadé [Igbo]

Mwê planté shu mwê
li turne ba legé
Ovid-o, bagadé, bagadé, eh—he

Mwê planté shu mwê
li turné maljo-jo (melangen, balissé)
Ovid-o, bagadé, bagadé, eh—he

I plant tanya
and it turns to nothing
Ovid, don't be afraid, don't be afraid

I plant tanya
and it turns to fear (eggplant, bush)
Ovid, don't be afraid, don't be afraid

The following song is one of the most beloved in the Nation song repertoire. Despite its fatalistic tone and expression of abandonment, it is danced
with merriment in the modern ritual. Among the Igbos, being without parents
was considered a dire state of isolation and loneliness, and having lost family
or being separated from them was the cruelest punishment. "Ba t'ni mama"
("I have no mother") is a recurrent phrase in the Francophone Caribbean
song literature.

Igbo Ginade [Igbo]

Igbo Ginade-o,
Tewé mwê kuma mwê
Igbo Ginade-o,
Tewé mwê kuma mwê
Igbo Ginade-o,
Tewé mwê kuma mwê
Ba t'ni mama
Tewé mwê kuma mwê
Ba t' ni papa
Tewé mwê kuma mwê

Grenadian Igbo,
Bury me as I am
Grenadian Igbo,
Bury me as I am
Grenadian Igbo,
Bury me as I am
I have no mother,
Bury me as I am
I have no father,
Bury me as I am

(continued)

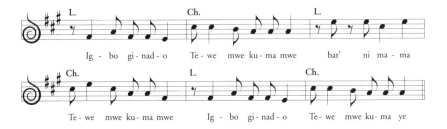

Ig - bo gi - nad - o   Te - we   mwe ku - ma mwe   bat'   ni ma - ma

Te - we   mwe ku - ma mwe   Ig - bo gi - nad - o   Te - we   mwe ku - ma ye

In contrast to the Beg Pardon songs of the warrior Cromanti nation, the Igbo songs present conflicted statements—at once uncompromising and defiant and then fearful. Igbos as a group seemed to suffer extreme homeland longing, a condition that created a huge mythology permeating traditional lore and colonial records as well. Historical writings, mired in the indifference of greed, document the Igbos as being caught in a state of "fixed melancholy." The Igbos were described further by Bryan Edwards in 1793 as characterized by:

> timidity and despondency of mind; [and a] depression of spirits. . . .
> [It] causes them an air of softness and submission . . . which [causes]
> then frequently to so seek, in a voluntary death, a refuge from their
> melancholy reflections. (Edwards 1793:76)

I suggest that the timidity and despondency assigned to the Igbo were misinterpretations of masked rebellious urges. Taken from a highly individualistic society, they were extremely perplexed at their condition under slavery. The only escape was their existential belief in an inseparable brotherhood that assured them the consummating return to their families at death.

The transplanted African often believed that at death his spirit would take flight, crossing the ocean, to join his brotherhood and ancestors. The flight of repatriation for enslaved people seemed to include the crossing of water and tracing in reverse the route of the Middle Passage. I return to the Bongo group to present a song that expresses the homeland longing encountered in the ubiquitous African/American myths of flight. More than any other, this piece suggests the theme of homeland longing and the ultimate form of rebellion in suicide by drowning that was often realized by the Igbo (Edwards 1793:76).

Oyo, Mama, Bel Louise [Bongo]
Oyo, Mama, Bel Louise oh
Nu kai ale na Gini pu
Kotwa pawa mwê!
Lame bawe mwê (Pearse 1956:5)

Oyo, Mama, Bel Louise oh
We shall go to Africa to
Meet my parents!
The sea bars me

In both versions of the "The Flying Africans" sketched in the introduction, the Igbos flew. In other versions, the interpretations vary, declaring that the Igbos walked on the water, flew over the water, or were engulfed by the sea in their efforts to achieve freedom or return to their homeland. Used perhaps by some to explain the sudden disappearance of runaways (Hamilton 1985:172), the tales take on individualistic characteristics and particularized structural imagery in each mode of flight. J. D. Elder (1988) tells of Trinidadian aviators levitating with corn cobs tucked under their armpits and people from Guyana explain the journey within a gobi—a gourd. In *The Autobiography of a Runaway Slave*, the Cuban raconteur Esteban Montejo explains the wandering of the soul as being like that of a snail that leaves its shell to go into another shell and then another (1969:131). In more detail, a Saramacan story tells of the practice of obeah or magic to enable walking on water and a parrot feather, properly prepared with supernatural powers, to actualize flight (Price 1983:112). In many stories a magical gesture, word, or song enables flight. But it is salt, the inhibitor of flight, whether instrumental in the stories or not, that is known to play a restraining role, disallowing flight, in all the geographical settings mentioned above.

Developed from the North American John and Marster folktale cycle, Zora Neale Hurston's folk fantasy "High John de Conquer" centers on the trickster figure John. He follows a slave ship to America "like an albatross" in order to instruct enslaved people on their power of flight and gift for music. With these they were able to ride a crow so large that "one wing rested on the morning, while the other dusted off the morning star" (1973:546).In the fragment of the story printed below, John de Conquer mobilizes the people and instructs them on how to escape. When they complained that their clothes would give them away as enslaved people, he responds, "Oh, you got plenty to wear. Just reach inside yourselves and get out all those fine raiments you been toting around with you for the longest. They is in there, all right, I know. Get 'em out, and put 'em on." The narrator continues:

> And then John hollared back for them to get out their musical instruments so they could play music on the way. They were right inside where they got their fine raiments from. . . . After that they all heard a big sing of wings. It was John come back, riding on a great black crow. The crow was so big that one wing rested on the morning, while the other dusted off the evening star. John lighted down and helped them, so they all mounted on, and the bird took out straight across the deep blue sea.

Norman Paul offers a Grenadian "Flying Africans" tale:

> At one time they used to make sugar and rum on Hamstead estate, but at that time I was not born. That was the time of my grandfather. They were Africans and they used to work at the time of slavery. My grandmother told us of the time of slavery, and when Africans were in Grenada. She showed us a mango tree in the yard, big as the whole of this yard here, where some of them went and gone up. They went into the cloud and they never see them again, they understand they had gone back to Africa. My grandmother said they were dissatisfied, so they went up the tree and away. (Paul 1963:16)

The inner desire for flight is drawn into metaphor and exquisite prose by one who had himself been enslaved. The following segment, inspired by the sighting of a tall ship, is taken from the slave narrative written in 1845 by Frederick Douglass.

> Those beautiful vessels, robed in purest white, so delightful to the eye of freemen, were to me so many shrouded ghosts, to terrify and torment me with thoughts of my wretched condition. "You are loosed from your moorings, and are free; I am fast in my chains, and am a slave! You move merrily before the gentle gale, and I sadly before the

bloody whip! You are freedom's swift-winged angels, that fly around the world; I am confined in bands of iron! O that I were free! O, that I were on one of your gallant decks, and under your protecting wing! Alas! betwixt me and you, the turbid waters roll. Go on, go on. O that I could also go! Could I but swim! *If I could fly!*" (1987:293; my italics)

From the vast array of structural variations and angles of flight, one senses at their core a single, powerful tale of return to Africa—a lament of mass suicide that may have grown from a historical incident at Igbo Landing in St. Simeon in the Georgia Sea Islands (McDaniel 1990). It was this history that Paule Marshall recounted in her telling of the tale. Whether the Africans rode in a calabash, floated in a seashell or on a leaf, soared on wings, mounted the back of a bird, or simply walked upon the water, they had to overcome the sea.

The song "Igbo Volé" parodies the flight of the thief, comparing it to the furtive flight of the Igbo. There is a play on the Patois words *volè* and *volé*, which mean "thief" and "fly" respectively. Said to be from Petit Martinique, this song is not a part of the Big Drum. It was collected from a single culture bearer living in Windward village, a northern district of Carriacou. Though it includes the Igbo boast heard in other songs, "ba ka fé Igbo," it may have been composed by Wally Bethel himself simply to please me during an interview on the Igbo. I include it because this is the way songs are made.

Igbo Volé Igbo [Petit Martinique]

I di Igbo volé
I volé passé Igbo
Ba ka fé Igbo
Igbo mandé
Ba ka fé Igbo
Igbo mandé

He says Igbos fly
He [the thief] flies better than the Igbo
Nothing can harm the Igbo
Igbos ask
Nothing can harm the Igbo
Igbos ask

Manding Songs

The next discussion features a song from the Manding collection—a favorite among expressive and intrepid dancers, who consider it deeply spiritual in tone. Possibly as a metaphor of the twisted-limbed Esu Elegba–type gate-keeper, dancers sway with a crooked contour in the lowest of the crouched positions that distinguish the Nation dances. The reference to the stick (baton) may be related to its use as Legba's phallic symbol in the Vodun dance (Courlander 1960:321).

Viola [Manding]

Viola-é, Viola-o
Ai-o, Viola
Viola, bam mwê baton mwê-o,
Ai-o, Viola

Viola, Viola
Ai-o, Viola
Viola, give me my stick
Ai-o, Viola

In the following song the meaning of Negesse Manding may be explained by a similar name in the Haitian Vodun. I suggest that Negesse Manding, like the loa Negesse Igbo of Haitian Vodun, is a Manding goddess whom singers implore to attend the ritual. *Sai Amba* in the last line of the text is another African-sounding name that inspired an etymological search. *Sai* may have grown from the Akan title *Osei*; Amba is the feminine Saturday day-name of the Fanti that Herskovits points to in a Suriname Winti song about which he states: "Here reference is either to a goddess or ancestress" (1936:540).

Mwê li-li-lé [Manding]

Mwê li-li-lé
Mwê li-li-lé
Mwê li-li-lé
Negesse Manding mwê
Vini ouè
Sai Amba

Mwê li-li-le
Mwê li-li-le
Mwê li-li-le
My Negesse Manding
Come see me
Sai Amba

Songs of the Remaining Nations

Some songs from the remaining repertoires reflect a pedagogical motive as in the Kongo song "Pwa Tululu," which teaches material survival in advising the substitution of the beach crab tululu when meat is scarce.

Pwa Tululu [Kongo]

Pwa tululu
C'est vivian-o
Kongo-o
Pwa tululu
C'est vivian-o
Kongo-o

Eat the tululu crab
It is like meat
Kongo people
Eat the Tululu crab
It is like meat
Kongo people

A second Kongo item, "Kongo Beké," gaily invites the plantation proprietor to the great "Crop-Over" feast at the mill: "Vini ouè mwê—mokai na mulé Kongo" ("Come see me—I am going to the mill"). Not only is the dance at the mill sponsored by the proprietor in this vignette, but even the new white dresses worn by the participants were gifts from him. Sugar Adams gave the following explication of "Kongo Beke" to Donald Hill:

> You have red man Congo, red people Congo. They say: "Congo bay key vinee (grenee) ma m'wa mo kai n'mu nay." They goin' to the mill, they run, dance, making the cane mill, they *fete* out in the cane factory. The wild dancing in the mill tonight, they giving *Crop Over*: eating and drinking, as today with the cotton mill there now (e.g., in 1971). That Congo is slavery time so they calling the white man, say, "Come and see my dress." They going to dance. *Big Time*, they say. Bay kay Congo, bay kay, bring the woman oh! Mogai na mulay Congo Oh grenee your woman oh. . . . So they call the white man that give the fete you know. . . . The white man say, "Oh, that's nice, that's lovely, a white dress!" The white man giving them that to go and *fete* in the cane mill. That what me, Sugar Adam, learn from my *Old Parents*. (1973:671)

This interpretation verifies that the dance received support during British rule (at least on the remaining French estates) and hints at the complicated and insidious relationship between slaver and enslaved, especially between enslaved women and proprietors, about which we would like more information. We can only imagine the subtle and conflicted rapport between oppressor and victim, engendered by their confusion at their mutual dependency and reciprocal distrust.

If the term *beké*, meaning "white man," truly had its origin in the name of the European explorer W. B. Baikie, the composition of the song above would have taken place long after emancipation. Baikie roamed the Niger region around 1854. New insight into the origin and date of the term's emergence comes from Kay Williamson (1984:102), who traces the linguistic variations of the term. She finds the word in Captain Hugh Crow's travelogue about his experience in Igboland before 1801. The term *becca* is found on his Igbo word list to describe substances associated with or introduced by outsiders: the *accobecca* (coconut) and *myabecca* (alcohol). Besides this, both Williamson and Trinidadian linguist Maureen Warner-Lewis (1991:169) trace the multiple etymologies of the word and its other forms (*bukra* and *bakra*) to the Ibibio and Efik term *mbakara*, meaning "white man; one who surrounds or governs":

Kongo Beké [Kongo]

Kongo!
Beké, vini ouè mwê
Mokai na mulé
Kongo!
Vini ouè mwê
Mokai na mulé
Kongo!
Beké, vini ouè mwê

Kongo!
White man, come see me
I am going to the mill
Kongo!
Come see me
I am going to the mill
Kongo!
White man, come see me

The single examples from the remaining nation groups, Banda, Moko, Temne, Chamba, and Arada, raise unrelenting questions about origins, the creation of language, the integration of cultures, and, again, the choices made by bonded people.

The northern Banda group rather than the Banda from equatorial Africa could conceivably have made up the Carriacou Banda nation. The Carriacou Banda song, sometimes called a "stranger's dance" (Pearse n.d.), may carry shreds of evidence to ascertain the locality of the Banda nation. The northern

Ghanaian Banda, an Islamic nation, experienced Asanti raids in the eighteenth century and to this day offer tribute to the government. The name *Quasi*, used in the song, is a popular Akan name, and this would be consistent with the inheritance of Banda acculturated in the Asanti region. Yet the Haitian funeral dance, also called Banda, caused me to question the classification of the dance as a Nation dance. It was also unsettling that texts in the Banda song group are in English Creole rather than in Patois. To further complicate the issue, I could not find people who claimed Banda ancestry. My culture bearers assured me, however, that Banda people had at one time existed on Carriacou.

Quasie No Dey [Banda]

Bayan-o, Quasie no dey
Yo-yo-yo Quasie no dey

Bayan-o, Quasie's not there
Yo-yo-yo Quasie's not there

Variants:

1. Me de me no de
La Quazi oh wo-yo
Me de me no de-o
La Quazi oh wo-yo
Me see me no see (Pearse n.d.)

2. Dem a call me-o
Quasheba dem a call me-o
Ai Banda dem a call me
Wy—you no yearie day (Pearse n.d.)

3. Banda call me-o
Quasi call me-o
Quasi-Banda call me-o
Oh yo, me no heari-o
Oh, me no heari-o
Quasi-Banda me no hear-i-o (Pearse n.d.)

The Moko song below simply states (if interpreted literally and as a Patois lyric) that "the hoe is not sharp." In stark contrast to this, however, the words *filé, na filé* occur in a Haitian song to describe the undulating motions of the snake deity Damballa (Courlander 1960:88). Given the commercial slave trade between Carriacou and Haiti and the congruencies already speculated upon with Haitian dance materials, this information may be broadly interpreted to place this song in the realm of the sacred and the words as evolved from African language sources.

U Mwê [Moko]

U mwê, oh, u mwê
U mwê ba filé, mama

My hoe, my hoe
My hoe is not sharp, mama! (Pearse 1956)

Pearse (1956) describes the Temne song below as:

a corrupt and half forgotten version of a song about the embarrassment of two Temne girls, Jeanni and Zabette, in trying to speak Patois correctly soon after their arrival from Africa. In the song from which this seems to have come the girls walk past a cross-roads, where the men assembled there greet them with various remarks. The girls do not understand what is said, and pass with their heads in the air. One of the men explains that the greeting was friendly. Reassured, they reply: "*Dende wa kuna ma bini wana,*" meaning "*Demî, demî mwê vini ouè u*" ("Tomorrow I am coming to see you").

Zabette Lundy [Temne]

Ah, ha, ha
Couma u fé, u fé
Zabette Lundy
Ah, ha, ha
Couma u fé, u fé
Zabette Lundi
Ai, Jimmy Lundy
Zabette Lundy
Couma u fé, u fé
Zabette Lundy (Pearse 1956:3)

Ah, ha, ha
How are you, how do you do?
Zabette Lundy
Ah, ha, ha
How are you, how do you do?
Zabette Lundy
Oh, Jeanni Lundy
Zabette Lundy
How are you, how do you do?
Zabette Lundy?

The secular quality of Zabette Lundy seems to permeate the performance of many songs, especially that of the next example from the Chamba repertoire. However, I found a linguistic clue that links Chamba Dumphries to ancestral beliefs. The term *Amba* (also heard in many songs as *amma, amba da, amba la, amba dabio,* and *abadino*) in the following song is the specifically Fanti Saturday day-name and the name of a female deity. Its phonological coincidence with the French word *amba* (meaning "under") may have shifted the meaning of many songs taking the interpretation out of the spiritual and into the secular. *Amba la* in this song is thought of as a Patois phrase meaning "down there."

Dumphries, mentioned in the song, was one of the largest plantations on Carriacou comprising in the 1790s a total of 698 acres and housing 352 enslaved persons (Slade 1984:486). Along with two other large estates, Craigston and Limlair, it housed more than half of all the enslaved people on Carriacou—1,865 persons. Cotton was probably its chief export, although indigo, limes, coffee, and cocoa were also produced. The three plantations were owned by George McLean, a self-styled governor of Carriacou and colonel of the Carriacou regiment; he presided over or served as a member of several influential groups in Carriacou: the Commission of the Peace, the Society for Promoting Christian Knowledge, and the Tree Planting Society. In this song, presumably initially sung by McLean's Dumphries plantation workers, the statement appears as a pleasantry—"how are you"—but the greeting may be have been directed to the goddess, Amba:

Chamba Dumphries [Chamba]

Chamba Dumphries-o
Cuoma yé, yé yé
Chamba Dumphries-o
Cuoma yé, yé yé
Chamba Dumphries-o
Cuoma yé, yé yé
Chamba Dumphries-o
Cuoma yé, yé, Ambala!

Chamba Dumphries-o
How are you?
Chamba Dumphries-o
How are you?
Chamba Dumphries-o
How are you?
Chamba Dumphries-o
How are you, Ambala!

Dahomey, the empire that was the territory of the Arada, is clearly saluted in the next fragmented Arada song. However, the full meaning of the song is not accessible. The character Derika may have been a runagate, taking flight and hiding in the woods:

Derika [Arada]

Derika-o, Derika
Derika-o, Derika

Wai-o, Dahomey
Derika!
Mwê tuvé Derika,
Gwa bois Derika-o
Derika!
Dahomey

Derika, Derika
Derika, Derika
Wai-o, Dahomey
Derika!
I find Derika
In the woods, Derika
Derika!
Dahomey

Clearly, religious practices have altered, giving new meanings to these ancient songs. Although there is no acknowledged spirit-world hierarchy at this
time, nor is religious possession an institutionalized part of the Big Drum observance in Carriacou, such conventions may have at one time been practiced. In Haiti the *loa* is thought to be invoked by ritual music, to mount or
ride the devotee who, in an altered state, expresses the personality of the spirit
"rider" (Deren 1953:29). In the Big Drum textual references to healing (as in
Cromanti Cudjo) and the moribund ritual pantomime of the Coupe Cou
lend credence to the existence of spiritual practices now lost to the ritual that
frames ancestral veneration rather than the worship of godheads like those of
the Orisa rituals. However, at some point the ancestral focus of the religion did

shift to absorb godheads like Oko, Negesse Manding, Anancy, Amba, and Iama Igbo Lele from various African practices.

I hypothesize that, like the appropriated deities, several of the untranslatable words found in the Big Drum Nation song texts survive as remnants of divine pantheons or ancestral units. Thus, Ena, Mama Nu, Salamani, Sari Baba, Sai Amba, Ahwusa Wele, Pa Beni, Kanjurio, Kanbera, and Abadino may be designations of spiritual consequence whose meanings were concealed or suppressed in the colonial Anglican world of Carriacou.

The eighteenth-century trade contact between the Asanti and northern Muslims, the Arabic-influenced Mende of the Mandingos, the language diffusion of Hausa speakers based on neighboring Trinidad, and the Arabic-infused Yoruba speech of the Grenadian Yorubas support my Arabic/Hausa translations. Though I have attempted to unravel the interwoven origins of these songs, it is premature to hypothesize further on the context or cultural sources of the remaining recondite ritual phrases.

The meanings of many Nation songs remain unfathomable in their parabolic settings, but elements of religious supplication and ancestor veneration appear dominant. The fragmented spiritual messages are charged with possibilities of alternative and conflicting interpretations or, in most cases, with indeterminate meanings. In African-based liturgies, a religious center inextricably links all aspects of life and, as in the case of the Big Drum, forms a new basis for encoding societal norms, restraints, and privileges.

The interpretations offered here imply the gathering of salient themes in ancestral dances. I suggest further that the laments, prayers, and praise songs that served as the focus of the religious dances of bonded folk, mixed with pragmatic themes, served also as instructions for survival, runaway alerts, rebellion messages, and consolation songs for the dilution of alienation and fear. Any interpretation of dance, aesthetics, music, and literature of the African diaspora should begin with the assumption that religious practice, political struggle, and the search for social mediation and justice share similar metaphors in the thinking of oppressed people.

Two

Sleepers Awake!

> Get up, it's daybreak, get up!
> Get up, it's daybreak, get up!
> But the morning star deceives me
> But the morning star deceives me
> The moon fools me—it is night—
>
> —"Levé Jou' 'vé ju'," Big Drum Hallecord

A t one time the Igbo nation danced only to Igbo songs and Manding people sang only songs that were accompanied by the Manding drum rhythm. But as the function of the dance evolved, accreting a newly formed Creole repertoire (Pearse 1955:35), dancers shared the songs and dances of nations other than their own. As time advanced, the various musical and ethnic strains merged, resulting in the loss of specific national characteristics. In this chapter I describe the lineage system, genealogy, and social organization of the people who left the imprint of their lives on the musical structure. In addition, I search out the symbols of performance and the Creole dance/song aesthetic of nineteenth-century free people, who had by then adapted new meanings in salt, food, dance, the drum, social structure, and lineage.

Some people lost their particular West African identity to the integrated Creole society. However, for those who were without historical knowledge, a means was instituted through which to reestablish national community. Whatever nation rhythm inspired the alienated could be embraced as that person's national code. Even today old heads declare that, if the knowledge of origin is lost, one may redeem it through a subjective attraction to a national rhythm. People are thought to be spiritually responsive to music and particularly responsive to the national drum beat that incites movement, produces sadness, or propels the person; the rhythm that stirs the emotions should be assigned as representative of the individual's nation identity. This was another principle (among the many accommodations the society created for the dispossessed) by which people whose mothers and fathers were dispersed could realign their African lineage.

In this way, music of the past perpetuated, reinforced, reestablished, and shaped not only personal identities destroyed by the slave experience, but helped to create new social and personal institutions. The social organization, patrilineal and to some extent polygamous, was no doubt buoyed and strengthened by the Big Drum.

The origin of the system of lineage is a lively issue of great importance in the literature on Carriacou. M. G. Smith, in discovering a patrilineal lineage on Carriacou and remarking on it as an unusual existence in the then British West Indies, suggested that the system could not be African because the founding nation of the ritual that commemorated the system was the matrilineal Cromanti. Given the malleability of family structure, the variegated definitions of African lineality, and the ineffable meaning of "African," a discussion of Smith's claim could occupy several chapters.

Smith explains the Carriacou kinship system as comprising large groupings called "bloods" that constitute four generational kinship segments. These lineage segments may embrace deceased members as lineage heads and are governed by the oldest male entrusted with decision-making and leadership roles. The code demands that junior men hold obligatory relationships to their elders and prohibits marriage within the group. Within the scheme of "blood" relations, although sisters' children are of the same family, they are not considered of the same "blood" grouping, because their fathers' lineages differ (Smith 1962a:267–77).

Among the Asanti, "it is the male parent who alone transmits his *ntoro* [*spirit*], just as they hold that it is the woman who alone can transmit her blood [*mogya*]" (Rattray 1927:51).[1] In traditional Carriacou the father was thought to endow the "blood" of family kinship; the mother merely bore the child. The discussion of inheritance on Carriacou takes on a fascinating similarity to the analysis of the Asanti mode, differing mainly in the identity of the transmitter of "blood." Ninety-five year old Marian "Mudder" St. John puts it metaphorically in terms of the drum:

> The father is the blood. The mother only bear the child, but the child come from the father. This is why it carry the father title [last name], it's the father that have race. That's why they say brother children must not marry, but two sister children could. It could happen. Long time it wouldn't happen, but not now. The boys and girls don't ask, they send and tell you they married. . . .

> The blood tells your nation. I wouldn't dance any other. I feel good for the drum tell you what to do. Move as the drum tell you. The drum is speaking, telling you how to get on, how to wheel, how to come back, work your shoulders. The drum speaking; without it you could do nothing.

Through the early works of Rattray on the Asanti, we find that the Akan were identified as matrilineal. In comparisons with American societies the definition of matriliny becomes clouded, demanding keener insight, refinement, and reinterpretation of Rattray's materials. Later analysts conclude with broader definitions of matrilineality (Murdock 1965:168), revealing more equal elements of descent in Akan society than were formerly recognized (Fortes 1960:253). Researchers who continue to reexamine the implications of broad terminologies and the definition of lineality now question a rule of descent that excludes the inheritance of spiritual and cultural knowledge (Robertson 1983).

The argument surrounding lineage arises primarily out of Smith's presentation of the "fact" of Akan matrilineality to refute the plausibility of the patrilineal Carriacou lineage system as an African type. For him, the matrilineal code of the Cromanti as originators of the Big Drum weakens the hypothesized African basis of the system (Smith 1962a:313). His argument narrowly assumes a direct, untransmuted inheritance of systems. Hill unearths and neatly describes two distinct lineages, the female principle and the agnatic, that Smith, in his 1953 research, saw as one. Donald Hill found in this a "striking similarity" in the ideology of descent and marriage between twentieth-century Asanti and Carriacouan people (D. Hill 1977:314).

Amid the controversies surrounding African retentions and the multiple processes of continuity, I offer yet another acculturation process, the reversal. The Cromanti shift from matriliny to patriliny illustrates a case of reversal. Reversal, as I see it, is an adaptation that manifests itself in the exchange of roles in social relations. In another sense, this reversal may be seen simply in the ascription of the word *blood* to the male domain rather than, as in the Asanti literature, to the woman's. In this instance it is the rubric that shifts and not the concept surrounding it. But essentially it is the conceptual embellishment surrounding the shifting ownership that evidences and connects the restructured trait to its original form; it is the logic upon which the regenerative soul/blood duality rests that attributes Akan qualities.

Given the mosaic of cultural choices among the nine-nation slave population, myriad transformations must have occurred to create the transposed society. To see the true character of the formulations we look beneath the external forms and regard the selection process, the ideal and application of lineage type. Cultural attitudes often lie on deep submerged levels, lingering indelibly and unseen. I therefore suggest that among the patterns of acculturation (continuities, reinterpretations, syncretisms), complete reversals in form take place, and within the creolized reversals the original ideation may persist.

When one categorizes a universal and multiform item like, for instance, a drum, one deciphers the large body structure, markings, design, and configurations on the body of the instrument as well as its performance style before declaring its cultural association. In the same way, I propose that, to reevaluate what was called "Africanisms" in the literature decades ago, we search for minute conceptual clues. This method rests on the assumption that mental grid patterns linger in the memory and may be called upon to reinterpret and even reverse earlier systems. Such an assumption promotes the premise that though patrilineal form overtook the African matrilineal code of the Cromanti in the Americas, the African base of the kinship organization was not altered, nor were its meaning and ancillary configurations weakened.

Charles Keil shows in his study of the Tiv that culture patterns may persist in the imagination to create reflections that impact upon changing art forms and social dynamics (Keil 1979). The holistic diagram below details the interconnectedness of structural entities and also the generative flow between culture patterns and cosmological thought. The positioning of the elements on the outer circle do not imply a closer receptivity of one domain to another.

The Carriacou family structure as reported by Smith does not cohere with the cultural facts of the 1984–94 L'Esterre community. My sampling of culture bearers of that district reveals no clear definitions or differences in the notions of "family," "relative," "race," "nation," or "blood"; these conceptions, outlined by Smith (1962a:194, 268, 303), have become uncertain, confused, and arbitrary. Genealogical knowledge alters through the years.

In the same way that Marian St. John employed the drum symbol to explain social order, knowledge of origin among Carriacouans appears related to and in some way dependent upon association with and exposure to the Big Drum experience. When questioned on personal origins, the Carriacouan might explain her loss of family history by reason of inactivity in the Big Drum, where origin, as well as incidents of historical record, are learned. Pedagogy in the dance includes not just movement, drum rhythms, classifications of dance

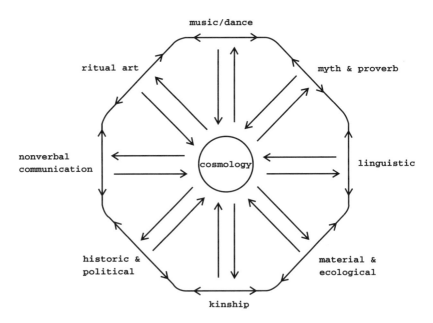

8. Holistic diagram.

styles, and Patois song texts but also some knowledge of personal and family legacies.

The social setting in the patrilineal society has slowly transformed itself and with that modification the necessity for strict male governance has, to some extent, waned. With the growing acceptance of female migration, which generates a more balanced male/female population ratio, the need for harsh absentee male control is precluded. However, attitudes formed in and by the past tend to continue. Male dominance is celebrated in almost all formal social rituals, and male empowerment continues to be the overtly accepted pattern in family and social life in Carriacou.

Though it is not clear in what form or to what extent the ritual organization of the past carried over into the material and social orders, or to what extent the social mores influenced the dance practice, there is no doubt that kinship organization helped frame the ritual construct. In turn, the ritual refreshed and proclaimed the spiritual ideology of the ancestor as family segment head. Whether conceived as African or Caribbean, syncretized or reversed, this system was erected by people whose dance aesthetic, ritual symbols, and dual generative concept tell us that *"their bodies were here but their minds were in Africa."*

The Mediation of Symbols

The dance and the symbols surrounding the dance should in some way elucidate the cosmology mediated by the Big Drum. Because the ancestors are the invited guests for whom the event is staged, the dances include the beloved dances of the past, from the era when the spirits enjoyed life on earth. Consistent with the purpose, new compositions of dance or song are not a part of this program; there is every effort to retain the ancient repertoire intact as well as protect the dance aesthetics from change. The historicity of the event is thereby balanced upon the single aspiration of entertaining the old parents. I will explore the dance aesthetic and the symbolism in the ritual and in the Creole song/dance form the Hallecord.

The double towels employed in the initial segment of the dance convey a powerful significance not fully defined by Carriacouans. More than "giving shape" to the dance, or substituting for sticks, flags, or wings of flight, the towels picture directionality in the universe. After each family member concludes a short, mediative, free-style dance, she/he stretches the two towels over one another on the ground. They form a configuration representing the crossroads that intersect heaven and earth, outlining the path for the incoming spirits. The four corners of the towels create the Kongo cosmogram representing North, South, East, and West, the cardinal corners of the world (Thompson 1984:108). The points of navigation are signified in the same way by the rum libations thrown in four corners of the site. In the Big Drum practiced in nine-teenth-century Grenada the ceremony took on a deeper spiritual tone than in contemporary Carriacou ritual. The founder and spiritual leader of the Grenada sect known as Norman Paul's Children, describes the invitation of spirits in the Grenada Nation dance and the general concern with the spiritual universe:

> They sprinkle rum in their yard and they go about with the spoon [playing the old hoe] right around the ring, calling the spirits with them. They leave the ring open, they leave a road from the East leading to the West and one from the North to the South. The purpose of the road is to say the spirits would come in and dance first, the dead spirits, the old people; they would call spirits both in the father's and mother's family, and they beat this three rounds before anybody could come in and dance. (Paul 1963:32)

The sound of the African bell-gong, made by the old hoe, attracts the air-borne spirits, and in the act of "wetting the ground" libation is offered to the ancestors as they appear. Jack Iron, the 180 proof rum, used in ritual as well as in social and serious drinking, entices and satisfies the spirits. Its strength is equated with that of the African parents, whose special mental "science" over-came the barriers of the sea in their homeland return. But alongside this mystical power the ancestors retain human qualities, for they eat, drink, dance, and seek pleasure just as humans do and with as much delight as the living. As people ingest the strong, burning liquor and quickly chase it with water, so, in the ritual libation, the male host throws rum on the earth and his consort following him cools the earth with water. In public as well as in private settings the foreparents may be remembered, libated, and addressed in this way:

> Toute papa mwe, mama mwe
> Pense mwe, Moka bwe mpe wum
> Toute monde pwa sa ava
> Moka bwe tu

All me fathers and mothers
Think of me. I will drink a little rum
Everyone come and take this rum first
I will drink also (Lawrence 1984)

Jack Iron rum arrives on Carriacou contained in large barrel casks hauled mainly from secretive and illegal ports—St. Barts and Trinidad. Shop owners siphon out the cask into smaller bottles for sale; when they are empty, the large wooden barrels are dismantled. They shave and cut the slats for the construction of smaller wooden kegs. The new barrels serve as the bodies of the *boula* and the *cutter* drums. And in the same way that the cask serves dual purposes, so too does the hot Jack Iron double its function as a medicinal balm when used as an external liniment for sore joints and muscles.

Food as well as rum accompany the dance as ritual elements. They serve as appropriate gifts for ancestors who are thought to enjoy the same recreation as the living—they eat, dance, and drink with the same pleasure as those who entertain them. Because of this, the parents' plate is set for them and guarded against poachers who might destroy the elaborate table.

All guests are fed during the *saraca* intermission of the Big Drum. Even though the late evening dinner is performed casually and seemingly without significance, the giving of food is a major symbol of a unified, compassionate society. Food distribution, "feeding the children," has ancient religious implications and a long African tradition. The root words *sadaka* in Arabic and the Hebrew *zedaqa* originally meant "justice," then evolved to mean "alms" (Mauss 1967:16). The tradition may be seen in modern Hausa beggars in northern Nigeria who solicit by calling out the culturally significant word.

Food as symbol extends beyond ritual in operating among the living in cycles of giving as a major social metaphor insinuating connectedness and friendship. It is admired as beautiful. At rituals the "smoke food" cooked over a fire within a three-stone border means goodwill, and at picnics people jokingly call their lunch pails *saraca* or *salaca*, imitating the ritual context and thereby eliciting a significant bonding in the act of sharing food. Cooked food is often exchanged between friends and accompanies visitors who are, in turn, supplied with an exchange gift. Whether it is a bag of limes or a fine breadfruit from the bearing tree in one's yard, the gift carries more meaning than its monetary worth. It initiates friendship, molds the sequence and times of visitations, and shows regard, affection, and love. The metaphors surrounding food giving hold meanings that have been shaped in the same way that the barrel was reshaped into the drum. And similarly, social ascendancy was framed and ritualized with experiential values, re-created in recycled form, and ceremoniously returned to the society as social codes.

At one time it was thought that when there is abundance, a portion of the good fortune must be returned to the poor, for greed and hoarding beget failure. The desperation of a man bestowed with extraordinary success and haunted by wealth is told in the parabolic narrative "Sallo," recorded by Donald Hill. The song has fallen into disuse, but people still remember the incident. The story as told is that Solomon Joseph was a successful seine fisherman of the Joseph family in L'Esterre village. On one occasion he hauled an enormous catch that was too large to sell. Much of it had to be given away. He was advised that his share of good was exhausted and that he would soon die. In response to this news he set out to repay his debt and appease the dissatisfied forces. As an avid participant in the Big Drum and Shango rituals he mounted these dances with sacrificial saracas throughout Carriacou, in Grenada, and on the nearby Sandy Island and Mabouya Island. After dispensing with his ritual obligations Solomon returned to Carriacou aboard his ship, dead.

Death may be caused by greed, an overabundance of the limited supply of wealth, insobriety, or the neglect of the spirit world. It is rumored that at a Big Drum Solomon had jumped into the free ring (the spiritual space that is reserved for the ancestral visit) and the spirits "threw him down." Solomon's unclassified song follows:

Sallo
Sallo, Sallo, Sallo, moka lay, oh
Sallo, Sallo, Sallo, moka lay, Sallo
Tama we vay
Kuma lay, kuma lay
Malay Mabouya sa memba guy
Malay ah ee bell
Sa memba guy
Sallo, Sallo, Sallo, moka lay, Sallo (D. Hill 1973:708)

Sallo, Sallo, Sallo, I will go
Sallo, Sallo, Sallo, I will go, Sallo
When I reach,
When I go, when I go

As I reach Mabouya the same thing
All will be well
The same thing
Sallo, Sallo, Sallo, I will go, Sallo

In his sacrificial fete Solomon had separate batches of food prepared especially for the visiting foreparents—a "parents' plate." The table bears cooked
items made up of the traditional foods such as coucou (corn meal), roll rice,
boiled plantain, fig, mutton, chicken, goat, and pork. Any type of food, fruit,
drink, and sometimes tobacco may be set on the ceremonial table for use by
the spirits and for the admiration of guests. At every dance edibles are dis-
played with pride on a white linen tablecloth inside the house.

The parents' plate must contain food from which salt has been withheld.
Because salt blocks flight, it is an abhorrent ingredient to the world of flight.
The widespread lore involving salt carries a great depth of meaning with varie-
gated practices distributed throughout the Caribbean and West Africa.

The precise connection between the African ideation encompassing salt
and that in the Caribbean is difficult to ascertain. It is known that in pre-colo-
nial West Coast Africa in the Sudanic and Saharan regions salt, gold, and cola
nuts had great utility, worth, and significance. As a major commodity and a
precious item, at times salt was exchanged for gold (Crow 1830:191).

Throughout the African diaspora salt protects against flying creatures by
obstructing their leapings, soarings, and freezing their flight: "The witch
leaves her skin behind on going out, and among the Vais it is thought that salt
and pepper sprinkled in the room will prevent her from getting back into her
hide" (Puckett 1968:155). Nigerian reports of the 1920s indicate that people felt
that malevolent spirits of sleeping humans prowled during the night. At the
presence of salt they succumbed and were annihilated, not being able to
reinhabit the body (Da Costa 1984). These beliefs mirror those of the Carriacouan people, who not only avoid the use of salt in the preparation for ancestral
flight, but who employ the agent against bloodsucking vampires of mythology.
The *lougarou* and *soucouyan* shed their skins outdoors and can therefore be
apprehended by spreading salt on the door steps, blocking the reentry into
their skin-clothing (McDaniel 1990:30).

A "new world" conversion in the meaning of salt may lie in experience
where the distasteful, salty and death-laden Middle Passage could have logi-

cally enforced the relationship between salt, death, and the spirit world. The sea is the physical barrier and salt, with its association with the sea, doubly inhibits return. It is the abstinence from salt that could permit flight, "confer special powers like those of witches," or even make one "powerful enough to fly back to Africa" (Schuler 1980:96).

Food in the eighteenth-century Caribbean was preserved in the sea-like brine that reeked of the infamous salt. Dictated by the Beneficent Clauses of the Code Noir and British slave laws, weekly allowances of salted codfish, mackerel, herring, or pork constituted the new, foreign foods of the enslaved. No doubt, the acceptance of salted food implied to the imprisoned workers an acceptance of bondage from which they could not "fly."

Along with this interpretation, a biological explanation may be construed for the symbolism of salt. The metaphor may have been rooted in the knowledge of the human reaction to salt—a bloatedness in the body. Symbols operate on several levels, suggests Victor Turner (1967:30), and often in polarized dimensions. There may be a "sensory" pole in the generation of meaning, having an easily recognized, physiological and affective frame as well as a larger, "ideological" pole. The physical connection to heaviness and groundedness is clearly recognized as the sensory interpretation, but the more recondite, cultural, and mythological meanings are more difficult to trace. Within a culture and even within a single culture bearer the polarized points of a symbol or a tale tend to mingle and bear multiple interpretations and, like the great myth of flight itself, deliver contrasting information to individuals.

One finds multiple ranges and levels of belief, values, and attitudes in the interpretation of ritual symbols. Some practitioners of the ritual "wet the ground" to nourish or appease the spirits who have flown away. Others, who do not fully accept the notion of spirit flight, may nevertheless wet the ground in an act of reverence, duty, or as an obligatory social necessity. Many people see the act as a critical feeding of their own memory and a revitalization of a personal spiritual inheritance. "What better way to remember someone than in the duty of feeding them?" suggest culture bearers.

Dance symbols also point to flight. The bird-winged outer skirt of the dancer, when extended, exposes the white underslip and resembles, for many, the white breast of a bird. Dance historian Beryl McBurnie, whose initiative inspired the revival of Trinidad dance in the 1950s, sees the bélè dancer as a tropical bird in flight with her "frilly petticoats, like soft down" and "plumes of rich plaid" (McBurnie n.d.:26).

The Frivolous dances imitate the courtship display of grounded birds—the hen and cock: the hen stops when the cock attempts to approach—and then she jumps and moves away. She stops again as the cock turns to advance and repeats the movement. The imagery extends into the female Creole dance duet, the *bélè kawé*, which suggests two hens fighting for a single rooster, represented by the male dancer who escorts the two female dancers.

But the dancers themselves, Estimie Andrews and Lucian Duncan, and older people with long experience of the dance express concepts of beauty developed from experience and from the memory of the last generation of dancers. Yard bird courtship imagery and allusions to flight permeate their descriptions of the dance:

> When May [May Fortune Adams] dance, that May used to dance! I don't know if you ever see those turkey cocks when they *kawé*. When she turn that way, when she turn that way, oh, she used to be graceful. (Mends 1983)

> They [the great dancers] always look like turkey-cock because they look brave, and you should make motion; you always look like something good to eat in the ring. It's beautiful. (L. Duncan 1983)

> When Collie Lendore danced, she danced cool—everybody stands with hands on hips to look at her. Not too much fuss and did intricate timing with her feet. (Hazel 1983)

> She dances like a top [MaTai]. People groan when they see her dance . . . was a sweetest dancer . . . a pleasant dancer. She smiles. She was always happy, always smiling, dancing. She's not this rough dancer. (E. Andrews 1983)

> Both top and turkey-cock enjoying, they not heating. Lose your time to admire them. If you busy you have to turn back and admire them. (L. Duncan 1983).

Allusions to the bird as well as to the top in motion are made especially in the description of the Creole dance, the Hallecord. It is considered an intrepid dance though outsiders see it as an elegant display in which the cool-faced dancer spreads her "wings" and soars. The dance name derives from the French *hale* ("to haul") and *cord* ("rope"). The combination of words refers to a move in the sport of top spinning. It is not the deft stroke of the wielder of the top that the dancer imitates, but the soft, stable whirl of the top itself with slight, cool bounces as she "sleeps." Taken with the beauty of this, the crowd at the dance cries out, *"dodo la!"* ("sleep!").

Even critical and negative statements reveal the dance paradigm of the past, the aesthetic of the cool, the grace in flight, the imagination of freedom. The following quote is from an old head who wished not to be identified.

> Today they don't dance with melody. *Long-time people* used to dance gracefully—not this winding [undulating hips]. . . . They are not beating or dancing as they used to dance. It's not peaceful anymore. They get vulgar now—winding! The Patois is the sweetness of it. They [the youth] don't have it.

From this I build a dance aesthetic from the elaborations above that reads: To dance with melody, grace, sweetness, like something good to eat, like a brave turkey-cock or dance like a sleeping top—that is Creole dance.

Whether through sound, sight, or name, the drum throughout the black diaspora refers to things African. With its potential for speech, for culture bonding and coding, the drum projects the memory of the Middle Passage and resistance to the scourge of slavery. Of all the preceding symbols and dance gestures, there is no more affective symbolic musical cue in this ritual than the drum. Its metaphoric and organological evolution in Carriacou is complex and recondite.

The drum trio of the Big Drum comprises the solo *cutter* and two *boulas*. They are all keg-constructed, open-bottom drums with goatskin heads secured by *wiss* vines or reed hoops wrapped in cloth. Modern variations, however, include the metal screw-type pins for tuning. The drain hole in the barrel drum functions as an acoustical opening—a sound hole.

The drum lends the ritual its name, *grand tambour* or *gwa tambu* (Big Drum), but today's drum is no longer, materially, a big drum. The drum sizes vary significantly. Its present height at 35.72 cm is a third the size of the drum heights reported by Pere Labat in 1724 that measured from 91.4 to 121.9 cm (Labat, quoted in Emery 1972:18).

The boula drum has dances named after it also. In Haiti, its name was taken to represent a dance event, the *bamboula*, and a specific dance style, the *baboula* (Emery 1972:158). Often associated with the word *bamboo* (Hearn 1890:144n.), the word origin, I suggest, is the Kongo word *boula*, which means

9. Lucian Duncan
and Donna Corion.

10. Two boulas.

"to beat." The remarkable description from Labat that follows informs us of eighteenth-century drum types, their dimensions, the straddled position of performer, and the musical function of each drum:

> . . . use two drums . . . hollowed to unequal depths. One of the ends is open, the other covered with a sheep skin or goat skin, without hair, scraped like parchment. The largest of these two drums which they simply called the "big drum" ("grand tambour") may measure three to four feet in length with a diameter of fifteen inches. The smaller one which is called the "baboula" is about the same length with a diameter of eight or nine inches. Those who beat the drums to mark the beat of the dance put them between their legs or sit on them and strike them with the flat of the four fingers of each hand. The man who plays the large drum strikes it deliberately and rhythmically, but the baboula player drums as fast as he can, hardly keeping the rhythm and, as the sound of the baboula is much quieter than that of the big drum and is very penetrating, its only use is to make noise without marking the beat of the dance or the movements of the dancers. (Quoted in Emery 1972:18)

The congruencies in the foregoing description of the Antillean drumming practice lead me to accept this model as the precursor of the contemporary mode. However, the comparison between the Carriacou drum ensemble and the Labat description reveals a few incongruencies: the size of the drum is now miniaturized, the drum's body is now a barrel rather than a hollowed-out log, and the drummer is seated on a stool rather than astride the drum. There is, along with these, still another inconsistency between the ancient report and the modern Carriacou style—Labat states in referring to the boula's function: "Its only use is to make noise without marking the beat of the dance or the movements of the dancers" (quoted in Emery 1972:18).

The obvious misstatement in the quote above on the lack of musical relevance in the boula should be disregarded, given the age of the description and the unfamiliarity of most missionary diarists with foreign music. By stating that "its only use is to make noise," Labat means simply that the rhythms were repetitive and not entrained with the dancers' movements. I chose the quote not to highlight the statement, but to gain information from it and introduce the extraordinary characteristic and the significant role of the boula rhythms.

Contrary to the "uselessness" of the Antillean boula, the rhythms of the Carriacou boulas are significant sound-emblems that resound the classification of national exclusivity within the social structure. In the ritual system each nation owns a rhythmic code, and it is the boulas that control the essential reiterative rhythm-fragment. It is above this revolving pattern that the cutter improvises, the chorus sings, and the people dance; it is the memory tool by which the people built their institutions and established their connectedness with the past.

Among the nine nation rhythms, the Cromanti is the most differentiated. In performance, after the chantwell and chorus introduction, the first boula enters, and almost immediately the second boula joins in on the nation beat. The second boula integrates his beat almost exactly with the first player's beat. The transcriptions in figure 11 are those of the nation rhythms.

We see in the Carriacou drumming practice an effort to isolate a specific drumbeat as symbol of national identity. Music was called upon not only to separate and distinguish people, but to operate conversely in unifying and bonding the pluralistic population. As the multinational society merged during the years after emancipation, the drum became the central focus of this plan.

In contemporary Carriacou there is secrecy surrounding the nation drum rhythms that evolved, perhaps, from an awareness of the long history of the system or from the sense of the clandestine forces historically associated with the drum. I speculate that there is also the fear of outside exploitation of the Big Drum that is now revived as a viable commercial vehicle for the two dance troops of Carriacou. Because of this, apprentice drummers as a rule do not invite interviews. But, more realistically, their reticence may evolve from the awareness that the nation rhythms are in disarray. At the death of the old head drummers the musical heritage was cut short and the art of drumming came to a precarious standstill.

Seated on low stools with their instruments stationed between their legs, the drummers execute rhythmic inflections with palms and fingers. In performance the cutter is always positioned between the two boulas with its open bottom flat on the ground surface. The two boulas, by contrast, tilt off the ground with the heads away from the drummers. Tuned lower than the cutter, the boulas' position (away from the ground) lengthens the resonating body of the drum cavity to lower the pitch still further.

The head of the higher-pitched solo drum is fixed with a string onto which

11. Transcriptions of nation rhythms.

pins are tied. These pins, operating like a snare, give the bold improvised statements brilliance. This same drum type, the *tambou, tambu,* or *ka* (*quart*), was described by Lafcadio Hearn in 1890 as made from a quart barrel. As with the Carriacou drum type, the bottom was left open, and across the head of the drum a "pin string" was attached. Rather than pins, however, this had thin fragments of bamboo or feather stems attached to it (Hearn 1890:143).

The etymology of drum names exposes a long and confusing linguistic interplay that parallels the transitional phases of colonial language usage on Carriacou. At one time the drums were called by the Patois names *coupe* and *fula* (*refouler*). Now the names are Anglicized and reinterpreted as *cutter* and *boula.* The relationships between the drum names *cutter, cut, cotter, ka, kata, coupe, tumba,* and *tambu* are, in fact, interlanguage translations that play upon antecedent words. These and related drum names are found throughout the Caribbean—in Haiti (*kata*), in Jamaica (*cotter, tambu*) in Guadeloupe (*ka*) in St. Lucia (*ka* and *tambu*), in Trinidad and Carriacou (*cutter*). The word *cutter,* I have determined, is the English translation of the Patois *coupé.* The extinct Patois term *coupé* ("to cut") was fashioned, I suspect, as a sound imitation and translation of the word *kata.* Thus, I hypothesize that the root of the mixed etymology is the Kikongo term *kata,* that means "to cut." Contemporary usage attracts other denotations to the drum name, but the English Creole action verb *cut* means "hit."

In its long historical usage throughout Africa, *kata* was most likely a significant word in trade languages, diffusing itself and appropriating meaning in several cultures. Among the several meanings of the Twi word are "to conceal, cloak, protect, or cover" (Barrett 1976:113; Turner 1969:106). In many areas in Africa, including East Africa, *kata* is the twisted cloth or circle of leaves used by women to steady and ease head loads; it becomes a personal symbol for the maturing young woman. The symbolism broadens in Jamaican slave culture where the twisted head pad, the symbol of marital unity, was cut in half at the divorce of a couple (Mintz 1974:217). Twisting the strands of a rope or a cloth strengthens the threads or fabric, hence the symbolic usage in the marital relationship. This physical truth creates a far-flung cultural proverb essential to the Zulu nation, a truth that promotes the coil, the twist, as a symbol of unity and strength (Werner 1925:110). In modern political struggles the metaphor emerges as the name of the South African Zulu political organization— *Inkata.*[2]

Social Structure and the Dance

Information on the social ideologies of historical generations surfaces not only from the interpretation of song texts and drum names. Dance names too express social codes. Gender, for instance, is coded in the dance style distinctions of Man Kalenda and the accreted Woman Kalenda. Similarly, the evolving nature of class comes through in the creation of a specific Moko dance, the Moko Bange. Originally the Moko Bange belonged to town people and was performed as a *bakra* ("white people") dance where "everybody dances in the ring together, instead of in ones and twos as in the other nation dances" (Pearse 1956:3). In contrast to this the Moko Yégéyégé belonged to Moko country folk, who danced singly and presumably with more traditional style. Though these dances are lost from the memory of the people, from the classification we glean a hint of the social differentiations among Moko people as well as others who adapted colonial styles. Similar accretions occurred in the Igbo, Chamba, and Kongo dances that spawned bakra-type dances such as the Jig Igbo, Scotch Igbo, Scotch Chamba, and Scotch Kongo. Pearse reports that the Scotch Igbo was a dance of mixed-race immigrants from Haiti (Pearse n.d.).

There lies implicit in the Big Drum categorizations of dance by race, gender, age, and nation—all aimed at social differentiation. The Woman Kalenda (newly accreted), the Kalenda Gwa Moun (a dance of the old folks gone before), and Bongo Sorti (a dance controlled by young people) clearly describe the gender or generation of the owners of the dance. Because the classifications are so neat, we may use the institution of dance as a guide to inform social structure of the past.

The following extreme and extraordinary example from James Kelly (*Voyage to Jamaica and Seventeen Years on That Island*, 1814) illustrates how the dance, for a discerning contemporary witness, was used as a mirror of group relationships. The scene is a Christmas feast given in an Antiguan Big House to which enslaved persons were invited. The Creoles mentioned in the excerpt refer to Africans born in Antigua.

> They took possession of the house *en masse*, with the exception of my bedrooms. Such a motley assembly! I had just formed such an idea of the revelry of the savages. The Mongolas, the Mandingoes, the Eboes, the Congoes, and etc., formed into exclusive groups, and each strove to be loudest in the music and songs, or rather yells,

peculiar to their country; and their dance, I must call it, was a display of unseemly gestures. These African groups took up the sides and corners of the hall, whilst the Creoles occupied the centre and the piazzas, evidently considered themselves entitled to the best places, which the Africans cheerfully conceded to them, evincing the greatest deference to the *superior civilization* of the upstarts! The one class *forced* into slavery, humbled and degraded, had lost everything, and found no solace but the miserable one of retrospection, the other, born in slavery, never had freedom to lose; yet did the Creole proudly assume a superiority over the African; and the Creoles danced to fife and drum, with a determination to be uppermost in noise as well as in place. The discordant assembly continued until late the following day.

The Antiguan pre-emancipation example above informs us of the structure of the early, independent nation dances, but more importantly of an early writer employing an intuitive research method long before the invention of sociology as an academic discipline. The dance described by Kelly reflects values quite unlike those of the Carriacou dance, which mediated against "classism" and toward a unified and more equal society. In the section that follows I attempt to reveal select social concepts and family structure of Carriacou through song texts.

The Hallecord texts of the Big Drum, composed during the post-emancipation era, offer a sense of integrated social and personal concerns. The focus in these texts is on relationships, the loss of family, consternation at nature and death—human concerns—rather than upon the communication with ancestors and gods. Despite the melancholy of the lyrics, the Hallecord was considered the "hottest" and most "enticing" dance that inspired even the disinterested to dance (Corion 1984). In the song "Drummer Mwe," a guest at the dance implores the drummer to play before the dance ends. She uses the ancient song words of petition: "My children have no mother to tend them."

Drummer Mwe [Hallecord]

Ai, vini mwe ka la bam mwe
Ai, drummer mwe vini mwe ka la bam mwe
Mama mwe, u ba ju ka ouvre pu m' alle
Ai, drummer u ba ju ka ouvre pu m' alle

Mama, mwe tini ish pa mama pu garde
Ai, drummer mwe vini mwe ka la bam mwe
Ai, drummer mwe vini mwe ka la bam mwe

Oh, come play for me
Oh, drummer, come play for me
Mama, don't you see that day is dawning and I must go?
Oh, drummer, don't you see that day is dawning and I must go?
Mama, my children have no mother to tend them
Oh, drummer, come play for me
Oh, drummer, come play for me

The next song commemorates the death of an old Kongo drummer, "Old Lazar." He died while the dancers and guests were awaiting his appearance and as they were "singing on him" for not showing up. The dance went on without him. The song words, dated by his death, were composed in 1888.

Laza [Hallecord]

Laza-a
Laza-o
Jou ka ou ve
Ba mwe Laza mwe? (Pearse n.d.)

Laza
Laza
Day is breaking
Where is my Laza?

The beautiful Hallecord "Fantasi-o" describes the behavior of people in love. As a parable, it tells of the nature of love and the sightlessness and non-hearing of those "asleep," in love. A young woman, Fantasi, is not able to hear her mother, father, or the rooster's call at dawn. She is in love, in bed with a married man. Although a dual system of mating, with several institutionalized forms, is (or was) customary, extra-residential mating is not the favored form—marriage is. "Friending," for instance, is a long-term relationship between unmarried people in which the couple does not live together—a form that may result in marriage. Modeled after marriage, there may be children in the union. In a second form of mating, "keeping," unmarried people (unmarried to one another, but the man having a wife) live together. The man lives in the woman's house with their children. In all cases the expectation is that she remain loyal to her mate; however, the male may be a married man in good standing. Although plural mating is somehow encouraged, all forms of mating outside that in marriage lie outside the rules of "decent" behavior and outside the parameters of the social systems reflected in the church and the Big Drum (Smith 1962a:192, 221). The song "Fantasi-o" warns against "keeping."

Fantasi-o [Hallecord]

Fantasi-o, etio yé
Na dodo yé levé
Na dodo yé levé
Fantasi-o, u ba tan Mama kwié?
Levé, Fantasi-o, etio yé?
Na dodo yé levé
Na dodo yé levé
Amba nom madam mayé levé

Fantasi, where are you?
Asleep—wake up!
Asleep—wake up!
Fantasi, don't you hear your mother's call?
Get up, Fantasi, where are you?
Asleep, wake up!
Asleep, wake up!
Asleep with a man who has a wife, wake up!

The next hallecord, "Sylvi ka Mandé," tells of a plan to travel to L'Abbe (Grenville), Grenada, and exposes the fear of living alone without family. Again the song words of petition are used: "Mwe tini sa papa pu gardé."

Sylvi ka Mandé [Hallecord]

Sylvi ka mandé ki la mwe rivé dans L'Abbe
Sylvi ka mandé ki la mwe rivé dans L'Abbe
Tombé mwe fuyé
Mwe tini sa mama pu gardé
Mes ami mwe tini sa papa pu gardé
Na L'Abbe, mwe di li
Tombé mwe fuyé

Sylvia asks when I will go to Grenville
Sylvia asks when I will go to Grenville
My grave is dug
I have no mother to take care of me
My friends, I have no father to take care of me
In Grenville, I tell her
My grave is dug

The satirical Hallecord "Lawen Victoria" was sung by free men who contemptuously parodied the intense search for indentured workers to replace slave labor. Beverly Steele (1974:27) notes that between 1834 and 1885, 6,207 indentured African, Indian, and Portuguese workers were admitted to

Grenada. However, no populations from these groups were brought to Carriacou. In the following song, *Coolie* (a word no longer acceptable), refers to the group of Indian laborers.

Queen Victoria took the throne in 1837, on the eve of emancipation, a coincidence that made her a positive figure and folk hero. She died in 1901, giving her reign almost the exact span of the entire period of active Big Drum composition. The Patois term for queen, *lawen*, permeates the dance ideal, song texts, and traditional acts. The people crowned a "queen of the dance" or *Lawen Juba* as a ruling symbol of the event. In the following Hallecord the singer satirically advises Queen Victoria, the importer of indentured servants, that when she buys a *Coolie* (indentured Indian), *Giné* (African), *Kongo* (African), or *Neg* (black), she should buy one for him also.

Lawen Victoria [Hallecord]

Lawen-o, Victoria-o
Lawen-o, Victoria-o
Si u kai gaé Cooli-o
Gaé youn pu mwe

Queen! Victoria!
Queen! Victoria!
When you buy a Coolie (Giné, Kongo, Neg)
Buy one for me!

Quashie Genealogy

To aid in the consideration of former and contemporary social concepts and family structure, I present the genealogy of the huge Cromanti Quashie clan surrounding Adolphus Osborne Quashie. The family history, unfalteringly recited to me by Henrietta "Nennen" Quashie Simon, commences with her great-grandparents, Mama and Papa York Quashie. In constructing this genealogy I have used the frequent age of marriage (twenty-nine, among Carriacou males in the 1880s) to mark the Quashie generations. Tracing three generations backward from the known date of birth of York's first grandson, Wilfred, we arrive at a birthdate of 1806 for York Quashie, and, given the calculated birthdates, Mama and Papa York evidently experienced slavery and witnessed emancipation in 1838.

The names of Papa York and his sons, Thomas, Simon, and "Prince" appear in an 1885 *Government Gazette* announcement of Carriacou water tax payers. Members of other Quashie families, including a Quashie Quashie, also appear on the list. Thomas Quashie, York Quashie's first son and the father of Adolphus, is registered in Grenadian newspapers as applying for a mare license in 1883 (*Grenada Government Gazette* 1883:30). The Quashies were prominent businessmen and landowners as well as artisans during this period. Thomas, a mason and cotton exporter with Grenadian business associations, purchased the 120-acre Breteche Estate, which is still owned by the family. The Quashie genealogy may be found in table 3.

The business prowess of Adolphus, the equally enterprising youngest son of Thomas, is shown on baptismal records in successive stages that indicate rapidly advancing economic roles. The records of his children's christenings indicate changes in his status—first as a laborer, then tailor, overseer, planter, and finally proprietor. His brother Winfred was a mason; Benjamin, a baker; McMillan, a carpenter; and Shepherd, a shipwright.

There is a great sense of pride within the Quashie clan of Carriacou, which sees its members as staunch Anglicans, educated musicians, and industrious craftsmen. Such self-esteem coincides with eighteenth-century descriptions of enslaved Cromanti people, who attracted praise for "elevated" souls, stubbornness, activity, and courage (Edwards 1793:63).

Quite in opposition to these testimonies of self concept, the West Indian usage of *Quashie* connotes the negative qualities of the bumbler and fool in

Table 3. Progeny of Adolphus Osborne Quashie (1885–1962)

Wife	Children
Rose Grace Simon	Agnes Theodora (Carr.), Peter (U.S.), George (Carr.), Dorothy (Eng.), Samuel (Eng.), Mary (Carr.), Frank (Eng.), Tom (Eng.), Victoria (Eng.), Alfred (Eng.), Edward (died), Phyllis (died)
Annie Robert	Veronica (died), Evalina (Carr.), Phillip (Trin.), Susanna (Eng.), Genevieve (Trin.), Carabella (Trin.), Jonathan (?); John (Eng.), Radix (Eng.), Queen (Eng.), Alice (U.S.)
Lena Quamina	Marlton (Trin.), Mathias (Trin.), Evadnee (U.S.), Uneeva (Trin.), 4 unnamed
Elega Fortune	Mathias (Trin.), Earlwin (Carr.)
Faith Simon	Oswald (died), Ende (died), Deli (Trin.)
Pet Colder	Roselia (?); Fortune (?)
Ati	(?)

Jamaica, Grenada, Trinidad, and Guyana (Lashley 1982:28). Orlando Patterson suggests that this negative view was taught during the period of slavery and projected by the slave master on to the enslaved person (Patterson 1973:37). The pejorative use of *Quashie* is seen as early as 1893 in Bell's *Obeah* (Bell 1893:69), where it is associated with the unlearned and unsophisticated black. The Quashie stereotype is analogous to that of "Jim Crow" in the North American vaudeville comedy duo, "Jim Crow and Zip Coon," representing the country bumpkin and the streetwise hustler.

In contemporary Carriacou by contrast, Quashie men are admired as black, tall, sturdy, and fondly described as ugly—an "ugliness" particularly attractive to women, my culture bearers explained, for they were "brave" (meaning smart), talkative, and very ambitious. Adolphus and his brothers danced the English Quadrille as well as the Big Drum.

The extraordinary Adolphus fathered thirty-nine known children with seven co-wives living throughout Carriacou, but reports estimate the total number of children to be more than eighty. Multiple mating in Carriacou was probably more prevalent in earlier times than now, for it is described as having been easier to support "outside" children then than now. The support of children is unquestionably and traditionally assumed by the father, who, if he is a sea merchant or captain, may sustain very widely dispersed families.

One senses little hesitation in the discussion of so-called "outside" children, and there exists an attitude of pride in the fecundity of the former generation. Two children of Adolphus Quashie and two of a wealthy Moko planter whose progeny are spread throughout the Grenadines spoke candidly on the subject of multiple marriage.

Adolphus's head wife, Rose Grace Simon, and Annie Robert and Pet Colder all lived in Mt. Pleasant, while the remaining four wives lived in Mt. Royal, Grand Bay, and Bellevue. In this West Indian family structure variant, the households are multiple and spread among four villages. Hill reported two cases of co-wives inhabiting the same yard or compound (Hill 1977:281) and that limited occurrence resembles the multiple marriage of African societies even more strongly than the example offered below. The list of Adolphus's children in table 3 also shows their routes of migration during the 1950s—to England, Trinidad, and the United States.

The scant baptismal records dating back to 1882 reveal no evidence of matrilineality among the Akan Quashie clan. However, had there been overt matrilineal practices, this would surely not have been reflected in church systems that, while not opposing traditional family organization, would have disregarded its existence. But even without clear-cut lineage ideologies, the symbols created by dance towels, rum libations, salt metaphors, the saraca offering, etymologies, African names, the bell-gong, drum and dance, and other obvious, expected African conceptual clues, it is "what people say of their origins, think about their connectedness and embrace as their tradition [that] remain(s) the most telling information sources" (Robertson 1984).

Three

Lavé Tete

Papa Legba, ouvri barriere pou mwê, la vie mande,
nou mande bien!

—Vodun Introit

I could only believe in a god who would know how to
dance; now I am without weight, now I am flying; now I
see myself raised above myself, now a god dances in me.

—Nietzsche, *Also Sprach Zarathustra*

In this chapter[1] I explore wider practices of "Danced religions"
(Raboteau 1978:15) that flourish with irrepressible force in the Caribbean and
that have spread their secretive nuances to urban communities to which Caribbean people have voluntarily migrated. They take their religion with them
to New York, Toronto, Miami, and London, but unlike the initial passage to
the "new world," their drums accompany them "to mediate, in a lived tension,
the experiences of separation and entanglement, of living here and remem-
bering/desiring another place" (Clifford 1997:255).

98

The calling, libating, petitioning, and veneration of flying deities of various nations and the adoration of distant ancestors are ubiquitous practices throughout the black diaspora. I shall draw on the classic, time-honored works (written from the 1930s to the 1950s) for this comparison of rituals to examine the spiritual systems of the Caribbean, investigating their intertextual bases in various places through time. The unity and logic on the various systems of dance resound in the naming of the rituals, in the personal access to religion that creates ritual and "invented traditions," in the grand metaphor of travel, and in the people's sincere regard for the world of spirits.

In Carriacou, ancestors communicate through "dream messages" delivered to members of the family when the time for a feast is overdue. The vision of an ancestor in a dream signals a request "to feed the children." Chief drummer Sugar Adams explained that he lived for dreams and warned me against ignoring messages: "Don't stiffen your neck and harden your ears, listen to what dreams tell you" (Adams 1983).

Culture bearers ascertain that spirits occupy a special place, a domain a mere partition away from the human world that may be embraced through rhythmic emblems, liquors, food, and accessed by song, music, and dance (Johns 1983). Ancestors and deities desire remembrance and insist that ritual functions be carried out; and to insure this, they threaten harm to those who ignore them or prevent their participation in the lives of the living.

Descendants of Africans in Puerto Rico, Cuba, Haiti, Jamaica, Grenada, Trinidad, Suriname, and Guyana have synthesized African spiritual practices in the new world within the Santeria, Vodun, Kumina, Sango, Orisa, Winti, and Cumfa religions. The St. Lucia dances Kelé and Kutumba, the Jombee dance of Montserrat, and the Nation dance (Big Drum) of Carriacou share places among the more dominant traditions that, to a greater or lesser degree, incorporate the African practice of danced religion. Even smaller, half-forgotten traditions like the Tobago Reel, the Gwo Ka of Guadeloupe, the syncretized Christian types of Jamaica (Revival, Convince, Pocomania), and the expanding Christian sect of the Spiritual Baptists of the Windward Islands speak to the ability and strength of the diaspora to absorb and sustain essential cultural habits.

In only one case is a dominant ceremony named after a specific deity, the god of thunder and lightning, Sango. Others, classed as "Neo-African cults" by Simpson, are named after the culturally specific concept for the spiritual force: *orisa* ("spirit" in Yoruba), *santo* ("saint" in Spanish), *vodun* ("spirit" in Ewe), and *winti* ("wind" in Saramacan). Similarly, the Cumfa (Komfo) of Guyana is named after Indian spirits (Herskovits 1936:61).

Taking the logical order in naming further, the *bembe* dance ritual belonging to Santeria, retains the name of a double-headed Yoruba drum. The bembe-type drums are not seen in the Santeria rite itself that celebrates, instead, with the hourglass-shaped *bata* drums.[2]

It is more usual that the drum takes precedence in the naming of ancestral events than dominant rituals. The *gwo ka, gumbay, tambu, tambo, kele, kutumba* and Big Drum are all ancestral dances named after the drum. I suggest that the wake dance of St. Lucia, *kutumba*, is related to a word used for the drum, *katumba (kata tumba)*.[3] Using the Creole drum *ka*, it celebrates, the death of an "Angol" or "Awondu" person. In a similar way I propose that the *kele* of St. Lucia, celebrated by Yoruba Ekiti, gets its name from the Yoruba drum *kele*. The Jamaican *kumina* appears to fall outside the pattern by being named after a dance style, *kumunu* (Bilby 1983:47). However, its alternative name, *ntambu*, means "drum" (Schuler 1980:77).

The Tobago reel, with its African behavior and possession practices, does diverge slightly in not being named after a drum but for an Anglo music/dance style, the reel. Also at variance is the Montserrat Jombee dance, that, like the larger rituals, takes its name from the spirits, in this case, called *Jombee*. The dominant religions and the ancestral dances are associated with either the word *spirit*, a drum type, or a dance style. The assumption of a historical religio/political role of the drum is widely held,[4] but from the itemization of the systems of naming we are further aware of the ubiquitous logic supporting the critical coherence between the gods, the ancestors, and the drum. And from this linguistic organization, an ineffable cultural equation may be drawn.

The events that I call greater or dominant rituals (the Orisa, Sango, and Santeria) have their origins in Yoruba culture. Vodun, too, though primarily of Fon (Dahomean) provenance, was significantly influenced by Yoruba religious thought. The larger congregations, then, worship Yoruba and Fon Gods, while the lesser rituals (lesser in power in performance and geographical extent) attract and venerate national and familial ancestors.

The basic performance elements in all the greater rituals are similar: cyclephonic texture employing three drums, rattles, bell-gongs, and antiphonal singing; a Nigerian or Dahomean pantheon with secondary Christian names;

libation, animal sacrifice, vèvè ground markings representing deities, cardinal directionality (that observes north, south, east, west), dance, and possession practice. In Santeria the care and feeding of the celt stones, the use of herbs as cleansing agents, and the saint Regla/Yemaya are highlighted. Within the Orisa of Trinidad, the dance and the employment of dance tools are essential ritual elements, while in the Vodun a profusion of chromolithographs of Catholic saints, flags, and vévé symbols exhibit its uniqueness. Each "new world" religion amplifies or interdicts a particular character trait of the selected deities, framing in singular ways the perceived essence of their personalities. From rigorous comparison of the ritual portraits of the Yoruba gods, painted by the people, I contend, further studies will reap critical information on individual pre-emancipation societies.

As we compare the Big Drum to the religions discussed above, it assumes a special place in that it excludes the element of spirit manifestation. Though it shares many qualities with the ancestral ceremonies, it is on the issue of spirit manifestation that the Big Drum ritual stands apart.

Though the colonial churches' impact on traditional cultures has not been studied in detail, the perceived contributory link between ritual survivals and the presence of the Catholic church has often been discussed. In Carriacou history the affirmative influence attributed to the Catholic church was shortened by the struggle for power between France and England, and the island, after more than one hundred years of colonial rule exerted in the French spirit of cultural compromise, encountered the colonial Anglican presence and its suppression of the meanings in danced religions.

Spirit Manifestation in Danced Religions

The distinctive feature that unites the greater "new world" rituals is the sequence of spirit manifestation, and it is the absence of this practice that isolates the Big Drum. In searching for a rationale for the desuetude of ecstatic practices believed at one time to have been a part of the Big Drum, one immediately focuses on the absence of the Yoruba, the nation responsible for the gripping, inspired, artistic and virtuosic spiritual behaviors in the greater religions mentioned above. All the major African religions in the new world have originated with the Yoruba or their neighbors, the Fon. Because of this, many people assume the Yoruba to be a profoundly spiritual nation. Actually, this nation may seem to dominate others in the potency of its spiritual legacy only because of its relatively recent influence in the new world.

Melville and Frances Herskovits described the behavior accompanying Yoruba spirit manifestations at a Trinidad Orisa feast as the Spirit Power "enters the head" and "rides" the devotee. According to them the preliminary signs of spirit manifestation are "the perceptible 'freezing' of the muscles of the face, the sightless stare, the twitching of shoulders and shaking of the knees" (Herskovits 1964:335). Each "entry" is danced with the particular wand or symbol of the invading Power—Sango's shepherd crook, Ogun's sword, Soponna's (Sakpata) knife, Yemanja's miniature oar or the ritual artifacts of other deities—a wooden anchor, whip, broom, or turtle.

Female as well as male devotees move beneath their personal deity and bear its symbol while exhibiting the personality and dance characteristic of the orisa "rider."[5] Although spirit manifestations are not performances directed to the audience, there is an appreciation of the artistry and a heightened experience for the observer at the exhibition of transcendental postures in flight. The body, with back erect, suddenly becomes supple; with bent torso the dancer takes long strides or whirls in a stylized movement. She may stop, with wide, vacant eyes looking forward, bend again, and then, with extended limbs, advance toward the drum. The devotee's face is transformed, expressing intelligence, beauty, defiance, or anger—as a mirror of the orisa, which has overtaken the ordinary face.

At the conclusion of each manifestation, the subject often "falls," now in a state of unconsciousness and under the control of the power. Water is poured on the head of the "horse" as a rite of consecration to the spirit in control.

Maya Deren comments upon the mediation between the drum and the devotee in the Vodun dances of spirit manifestation. She explains the control by the solo drum, the *maman*, which regulates the psychic tension by drum "breaks" that literally break the concentration of the vulnerable dancer, whose disengaged state permits the *loa* spirit either to be withheld or installed. Deren, an artist/researcher of Vodun, describes her rare personal introduction into loa manifestation during research in Haiti. She recalls being caught in a cylinder of sound and frozen by the perception of her leg being driven into the ground by the beat of the drum.

> My skull is a drum; each great beat drives the leg, like a point of a
> stake, into the ground. The singing is at my very ear, inside my head

. . . I cannot wrench my leg free. I am caught in this cylinder, this well of sound. . . . The white darkness moves up the veins of my leg like a swift tide rising, rising; . . . It is too much, too bright, too white for me; this is its darkness. (Deren 1953:260)

A second personal account comes from Marjorie Whylie, a Jamaican pianist/ethnographer, who informs us that during a National Dance Theater performance of a Kumina song something unexpected happened. She was playing an anointed shaker borrowed from the leader of the Kumina ensemble when she became oblivious of the arena in which she was standing and was able to observe her performance from a place outside of herself.

> Now a curious thing happened to me in performance: I was no longer conscious of the spot on which I was standing. I seemed to be observing myself playing from outside somewhere. My spirit, or whatever it is, left the body there performing, and I was up there somewhere floating. (Quoted in Logan 1982:93)

The divergent experiences described above may be seen as separate modes of spiritual flight. In the first, as described by Deren, the deity travels from his/ her habitat to invade "and dance within" the devotee. A reversal in the directionality of flight mediates the trance behavior of the second experience. Instead of the spirits traveling in, occupying the musician, she found herself "raised above herself" and transported outward. These are discrete experiences as indicated by alternative systems of flight; in the first the gods visit the subject internally, and in the second the subject soars mentally to the outer world.

Raboteau (1978:63) succinctly reviews Erika Bourguignon's analysis of the African and Protestant forms of spirit possession, in which Bourguignon compares altered states in the Haitian Vodun and the St. Vincent Spiritual Baptists. In the Haitian model the dancer and the crowd interact, with a large range of behaviors including impersonation, dancing, singing, smoking, drinking, eating, and even sometimes climbing trees. On the other hand, the Spiritual Baptist, in the state of altered consciousness, internalizes and turns toward personal interaction with the spirit.

For many in modern Carriacou, the ancestral ritual stands in opposition to fundamentalist Christian beliefs. Examples of this came from culture bearers with whom I spoke and, most revealingly, from a young woman after her conversion to the Spiritual Baptist faith. She explained her unanticipated absences from the Big Drum to me by simply quoting a popular biblical motto, Matthew 6:24: "One can not serve two masters: for he will hate the one and love the other." But in dissimilar circumstances I observed many people, including leaders in the Spiritual Baptist church, celebrating and affirming, with ecstatic behaviors and articulated statements, the spiritual/cultural relationships between the church and the Big Drum ritual. On the other hand, in a conversational tone, an older Seventh Day Adventist culture bearer introduced his personal dilemma and the moral implications of his continuing involvement in the Big Drum. On several occasions he asked me, "Is the Big Drum bad?"

The "Invented Tradition": Rastafarianism

Many conditions may have promoted ritual survival on Carriacou, but the complexity and ineffable quality of those variables make the assignment of the influences highly conjectural. Factors such as the foresight of women and men with a sense of historicity, the people's collective historical memory, the specific ethnic makeup of the African presence, the national history of colonial control, material culture, island size, ecology, and historical/contemporary missionary involvements may support as well as hinder continuities.

The salient factor upholding substantial continuities of African culture in the Caribbean is the influence of late-arriving Africans. Between 1843 and 1885, 6,207 "late-to-arrive" Africans entered Grenada as indentured servants (Steele 1974:27). It was this second wave of Africans that brought traditions to revitalize and renew the older, prohibited, and fading African habits. Interest in danced religion resumed on Grenada and Trinidad with the integration of the new Yoruba immigrants. However, as a consequence of the Yoruba revivals came the displacement of other original and competing dance traditions. This was the case with the Nation dance (Big Drum) of Grenada. At the revitalization of the Sango tradition in Grenada, the multi-ethnic Nation dance of Grenada was gradually overshadowed and finally lost (Smith 1962a:10). However, there were no Yoruba immigrants to Carriacou during this era (Smith 1965:34), and the Big Drum continued in Carriacou devoid of Yoruba influence.

We sense antiquity in the music and dance of the Big Drum and the Sango of Grenada, but Eric Hobsbawm suggests something other. Writing on the historical shallowness of certain traditions, he cautions against unfounded assumptions of antiquity. He states, "Traditions which appear or claim to be old are often quite recent in origin and sometimes invented" (1983:1). But even with this caveat it is difficult to accept traditions that appear distant conceptually and culturally, to be, in reality, newly restored and contemporary, living practices. In the case of the kelé of St. Lucia, it is believed that Ekiti/Yoruba immigrants brought the ritual there in 1867 (Kremser n.d.:82), making it a relatively new imported practice rather than, as often thought, a ritual surviving there over centuries. In the same way, Kongo immigrants brought Kumina to Jamaica between 1840 and 1870, much more recently than had been assumed. Beverley Hall-Alleyne (1990:39) underscores the "shallow history" warning with a comparison of Jamaican Maroon-language retentions and states that the Twi language of the original Akans was indeed a more archaic language variation than the Kikongo patterns introduced by the late-arriving Kongos. Similarly, Monica Schuler (1980:9–10), in her work on the Kongo indentured immigration to Jamaica, points to the incompleteness of survival studies, which ignore the impact of the indentured immigrants of the nineteenth century. She also assessed the renewal in Grenada fostered by indentured workers as a remarkable revival of ancient ritual practices. And, again, a congruent explanation is held by Bascom, who theorizes that relatively large numbers of Yorubas immigrated to Cuba in the 1830s after the Fulani conquest of Ilorin and Old Oyo (Raboteau 1978:41). But more than this, the importation of enslaved people to Cuba is known to have continued until 1873 (Fraginals 1984:5), making the Cuban case an example of protracted cultural fertilization. Though there is wide agreement among scholars from various disciplines on the significant influence of late African emigration, its cultural influence is still unclear, and the imported African tradition in the Americas of danced spirit manifestation is still viewed as an ancient and far removed practice.

As we compare the African dances to the newly formed expressions in the Americas we see elements of syncretism and alterations in symbols and meaning created through choice and invention. A truly "invented tradition," the Rastafarian Nyabinghi movement of Jamaica, came to light in the 1930s. Embracing the ideals of African repatriation and the overthrow of the "white man's Babylon," the major themes of the "new tradition" were political, moral, and religious. Among the practices that mirror ancient behaviors is the ancestral focus that places Emperor Haile Selassie in the role of "Highest Ancestor." The Kongo-inspired cardinal directionality, protective emblem-*guards*, such as the Ethiopian and Garveyite flags placed at gateways to yards, and the mystical drumming that is "said to 'draw earthforce—lightening, thunder, and earth-quake—from Zion to earth'" (Homiak 1993), reify ancient thought. Most convincingly, the abstinence from salt (see chapter 1) and the reliance upon dreams and visions unite this tradition with the collective ideologies associated with Caribbean ritual behavior. However, the Nyabinghi sect rejected possession, trance, and any involvement in *obeah* (mental control) in the founding theories governing the movement.

The theme of repatriation which registers prominently in Rastafarian songs and chants emerges as the essential theme of flight. The Rastafarian song below expresses the sentiment much in the same manner as the Carriacou Bongo song "Oyo, Mama, Bel Louise," which declares, "We shall go to Africa to meet my parents!" (see chapter 2).

> Africa I want to guh
> Africa I want to guh
> Zion is my father's home
> Zion is where I come from
> I, I, I want to guh (Homiak 1993)

Orisa of Trinidad

Throughout the diaspora deities took on mutated names and selected Christian counterparts, associating themselves with emblematic colors, favorite foods, habitats, and special feast days. However, the chief Gods (Obatala, Obalufon, Elefon, and Oduduwa) are not assigned Christian equivalents or earthly symbols. The Orisa powers listed below are those of a particular Trinidad shrine, reflecting the personal communication established by the flight of certain gods. Young adult leaders of the Orisa Yin Cultural Organization constructed a listing of the gods guiding southern Trinidad. The organization researches and reinterprets Yoruba traditions in order to revise and codify the materials. Their undertaking coincides with the 1988 movement that sought to change the name of the religion from *Shango* to *Orisa* (which means "spirits"). They felt that the term *Orisa* more properly projects the wide distribution of powers (*Orisa*) served in the assemblies. Table 4, a compilation by the Yin Organization, reveals them as an African-centered movement in their adaptation of Yoruba orthography and their commitment to cultural revitalization and documentation of the prominent powers of southern Trinidad.

Typically, Orisa feasts take place at the shrine compound consisting of a straw-roofed *palais* (a simple tentlike structure lined with benches), the *chapelle* (a small structure housing the dance wand-tools), and several *stools* or altars commemorating various gods. Flags bearing designs using the representative colors of communicative deities fly on tall bamboo poles over the compound, and candles burn on the ground near the stools and at the four corners of the palais worship space. Throughout the compound participants

Table 4. Orisa powers and Christian saint counterparts

Orisa power	Christian saint
Ogun	Michael
Oranyan	George
Aganyu	Gabriel
Osoosi	Raphael
Soponna	Jerome
Onile	Mother of the Earth (Mama La Terre)
Osanyin	Francis
Ibeji	Peter and Paul (twins)
Dada	Anthony
Erinle Ajaja	Jonah
Sango	John
Orunmila	Joseph
Obatala	Godhead
Obalufon	Godhead
Elefon	Godhead
Oduduwa	Godhead
Yemanja	Ann
Osun	Philomena
Oya	Catherine
Oba	Theresa

erect multiple symbols of color, gesture, and practice before the ritual. For the feast of Elefon, which takes place every four years and is hosted by Queen Mother Lindsey of Oropuche, adherents dress the compound in flowing bands of white cloth; and with the same care they prepare and bathe the three white bulls in herbal water, wrapping them in white capes before the sacrifice.

Music is essential and uninterrupted during the all-night feast. The drummers perform seated, now and then trading places with substitute drummers. They play with the double-headed drums on the thigh or, as with the smallest drum, stationed on a stool. Simpson records the varying sized, cylindrical drums as *oumehleh* (*omele*), *congo*, and *bembe* (*big drum* or *mama*). Only one head of the bembe and congo is struck with the curved Yoruba drumstick, while fingers apply pressure to the drumhead. The smallest drum, omele, is beaten with two sticks in fast, continuous, repetitive rhythms. Situated in the middle of the ensemble, the player of the largest drum (*bembe*), executes dramatic "slams" and virtuoso cross-rhythm statements above the sound of several *chac-chacs* (rattles). The three-member drum ensemble accompanies the call of the song leader and the monophonic responses by the participants.

Shakers, Shouters, and Spiritual Baptists

Fine examples of ritual syncretism are seen in the Spiritual Baptist religion. Within this religion the integration of Christian dogma and African ideology varies, placing each congregation along a charged continuum between the poles of Christian and Orisa practices, giving rise to several variations of congregations called Baptist Sango and Baptist Africans. Traditionally, members of the Spiritual Baptist religion come from the working poor, but there is a segment of "invisible" adherents of moneyed and intellectual classes whose connections to the church remain secret (Williams 1985:117).

The origin of the Trinidad Spiritual Baptist religion is unclear. It is known, however, that the Spiritual Baptists stem from the Shakers of St. Vincent, called Shouters in Trinidad, both titles portraying the ecstatic worship style of the movement. Among the theories of their original sources are the claims that (1) it evolved out of the Sango religion; (2) it came out of the Methodist movement arriving from Antigua in the 1770s; and (3) it grew from the American influx of liberated soldiers from the War of 1812 (Glazier 1983:37). Although song materials may have been appropriated from each of these sources, and especially from the spiritual singing of the Baptist " 'Merikans" (McDaniel 1994), the origins and date of the founding of the religion have not yet been traced.

Candles, flower-filled gourds, vials of perfumes and oils (altar fluids), a nautical steering wheel laden with candles, the Indian *lota* plate, and a bell are the most distinctive symbols of the movement. These symbols surround the centerpole, the essential symbol, "derived from the Ancient African church, represents the timber of Lebanon, which was used for the construction of Solomon's temple" (Thomas 1987:31). Spontaneous libations of altar fluids and bell-ringing occur there and at the cardinal points or in the corners of the room, punctuating and shaping the progress of the service.

The memory of legal suppression instituted against the early church in Trinidad (called Shouters) keeps the imported movement partially underground and vastly misunderstood. Instituted in 1917 and repealed in 1951, the Shouters Prohibition Ordinance:

> makes illegal the practices of the body known as "Shouters" and its provisions should be rigidly enforced by the Constabulary. . . . These practices include as follows:

> a. Binding the head with white cloth.
> b. Holding of lighted candles in the hands
> c. Ringing of a bell at intervals during meetings
> d. Violent shaking of the body and limbs
> e. Shouting and grunting
> f. Flowers held in the hands of persons present
> g. White chalk marks about the floor (quoted in Herskovits 1964:348)

Cultural amalgamation is obvious in the theology and music of the religion, which integrates Catholic ritual and many distantly related vocal types including Yoruba songs, Hindu chants, Chinese vocalizations, American spirituals, and Anglican hymns. These musical styles constitute the superimposed "sheets of sound" during the prayer ritual, the search for "power" (in this instance, mental trance), and astral flight. The language of the song texts resonates the cultural landscape of the journey, and the knowledge of the untranslatable languages is explained by a supernatural "connaissance" gained through the practice of mental travel. Travel is a central theme of this sect, whose songs express the motion of walking and whose language and song are filled with the imagery of flight.

Hindu Chant
Rt. Rev. Eudora Thomas

Songs and chants accompany a great portion of the Spiritual Baptist service, and often two songs flowing simultaneously may be joined by a third to form an inspired, free-form, polyphonic texture. Traditionally only hand clapping and foot tapping occurs, though in Sango-Baptist services drums may be used. The several song types and practices of the extensive Spiritual Baptist repertoire include lining out, 'doption, trumpets, and spiritual shouts. Lining out is a practice in which words of a traditional hymn are first intoned by a tenor song leader as a prompt for the congregation, which responds with variations on the melody. Trumpets and spiritual shouts are usually choruses that, like the 'doption modes, accompany the trance sequence.

The 'doption musical practice employs vocables to "adopt" an Anglican or Sankey melody into a fast-moving, harmonized, and rhythmically orchestrated song. During the singing of the hymn, syllables ("bi mi bim, bam bi-bi bim") slowly replace the words to imitate drumming; handclaps and foot taps in strict eighth-note rhythms accompany heterophonic vocal wanderings, grunts, rhythmic inhalations, and overbreathing in voiced rhythms, resulting in a jubilant and multi-rhythmic texture. Mervyn Williams notes that accompanying the spiritual practice of 'doption, the "journey to Africa," bird sounds may sometimes be heard interspersed within the language of glossolalia (1985:49). Other musical 'doption modes and practices inspire mental travel to China and India. Describing the wanderings of spiritual travel toward Zion, Reverend Oliver Charles says: "In 'doption you have different roads. If you going right, and immediately you turn—everywhere have a junction—and when you reach that junction, you have to know where you going to. If you going to the valley, going Zion, Calvary, Mt. Sinai, Mt. Canaan, valley of Jehoshaphat, Dry Bone, Antediluvian World" (Charles 1991). Pearse suggests that up to fourteen archetypal journeys match particular song types or 'doption modes

(Mayhew 1953:14). The 'doption tune "This Train Bound for Glory," transcribed below from a congregational meeting led by the Rt. Rev. Eudora Thomas of Trinidad's Mt. Carmelite Assembly, inspires travel to Africa.

This Train Bound for Glory

Congregation: This train, bound for glory
Leader: This train, this train, this train is bound
Congregation: This train, bound for glory
Leader: None shall enter but the righteous and holy
Congregation: This train, bound for glory
Leader: (trumping and vocables)

'Doption singing plays a part in the mourning ground initiation experience in which spiritual gifts are bestowed, metaphorically, like academic degrees. The supernatural "going to school" (Henney 1973:245) confers rank and status within the hierarchic church structure on the devotee. The season for the "graduation" is requested by the initiate, and after preparations are made, she is placed on the ground in an antechamber of the church. During the three-day, seven-day, or twenty-one-day isolation sessions of fasting, prayer, and song-induced dreams and visions, a personal mentor—a "pointer"—visits the initiate. The pointer guides the meditations and attends to the spiritual needs of the initiate. Later, at the conclusion of confinement, visionary tracts are recalled and recited to the congregation by the pilgrim, who has "risen" from mourning. From the first mourning ground and other subsequent initiations, supernatural "gifts" and duties as nurse, watchman, seer, teacher, mother, preacher, pointer, and doctor are interpreted, disclosed, and assigned by the shepherd of the church.

At the festive conclusion of the mourning ground initiation, members parade from the chamber of isolation to the church door singing with lifted banners. This representation of resurrection and awakening ends the isolation that empowers her/his spiritual life in the hierarchy of the church. Herskovits comments on the "mourning ground" of the Spiritual Baptists, comparing the rite of consecration to the head-washing initiation of the Orisa ritual, the dedication to the deity that has settled within the individual (Herskovits 1964:322).

Mourning ground visions include mental roamings, memory tracts of treks through vales and around hills that follow detours to arrive at the destination of acquired knowledge and the achievement of inspired gifts.

During the recitation of the trance/travel, the initiate simulates the action of walking, moving her/his hands (which hold candles), arms bent at the elbows, alternately forward and back. The pilgrim endures the restricted body movement for hours during the ceremony of exhortation and song. The movement continues as she/he recounts visions of the landscapes through which she traveled while on the mourning ground, describing the wanderings according to the essential cardinal quarters—north, south, east, and west—in narrations reminiscent of those outlined by Orisa participants for the roads traveled by arriving African deities.

The language of travel permeates the literature on the Spiritual Baptists, and the songs, too, project the goal of flight. "Lend Me Your Wings," below, still a major chorus in the services, was taped by Herskovits in Toco, Trinidad, in 1939. The early text was sung in a very fast call and response, repeating the first two phrases: "Give me wings / Let me fly to Glory / Only the pure in heart / Dear Jesus." The later version, below, sung by Grenada's Archbishop Edmund Gilbert of Holy Temple of the Unicorn Spiritual Baptist Church, is an extended form.

Lend Me Your Wings

Lend me your wings, I want to fly to glory
Lend me your wings, I want to fly to glory
Lend me your wings, I want to fly to glory
Blessed is the pure in heart, Jesus

Lend me your wings I want to fly   to glo - ry.   Lend me your wings I want to fly   to glo - ry.

Lend me your wings I want to fly   to   glo - ry.   Ble-ssed is the pure in heart   Je - sus.

Many Spiritual Baptists of Trinidad also practice Orisa as those of Grenada engage in Shango (Sango) observances. But more significant than this is that church members often visit ritual feasts as a congregation, accompanied and sometimes transported by their shepherd or pastor. When the Spiritual Baptist leader officiates at the Orisa danced religion, it is difficult to separate the specific theologies in the services, which forcefully intersect and borrow liturgical segments from each other.

Esu Elegbara and Dance/Songs

Though the Yoruba trickster deity Esu Elegbara plays no acknowledged role in the Spiritual Baptist religion, the introductory role associated with him is felt in the services. For instance, during the "surveying" process of the service, libation is offered at the four corners and doorways of the praise house, a practice related to Esu's role of preparing access for the spirits. I witnessed this ceremony during the dedication of a newly built Baptist church in Carriacou, where the corners of the room were anointed and named, with one christened Philomena, the saint-name for Osun, the goddess of the river.

In the older ritual, it is Esu Elegbara who opens the junctures normally blocked and it is he who, in many minds, eliminates the space between the spirit and human worlds. A complex, harassing spirit, he does not appear on the list of divinities in the Trinidad Orisa for he is not a personal spirit with the power to invade. But, nonetheless, he commands the service and attention of the shrine. His eccentric persona elicits an ostensibly negative response from the community of worshippers. They dismiss Esu soon after his arrival, partially ignoring his ambiguous status as deity, or, as in the kelé of St. Lucia, chase him out with his calabash of ash smashing it at midpoint or at the end of the ceremony (Kremser n.d.:91). Despite the apparent disapproval, his appearance at the commencement of the dance is essential to most Yoruba-based rituals.

Dunham interprets Legba (one of the many variations of Esu Elegbara) as polynational, serving, among others, Yorubas, Arada-Dahomeans, Igbos, Nagos, and Kongos as a gatekeeper or spirit intermediary between humans and true gods. But despite the universality and the significant nature of his domain, in Christian areas of Nigeria the Esu persona is conceived of as Satan. The duality of Esu Elegbara is seen not only in the polynational nature of his sovereignty but also in the ability of his congregations to absorb, syncretize, accrete, and reinterpret unrelated religious principles.

Religious syncretization in African religious thought has received a great deal of attention from early anthropologists. Melville Herskovits laid the framework of the processes of acculturation and defined the several levels of possible cultural changes in a group living within a major influencing culture. Retention (of old practices), syncretism (combination of two discernible elements), revitalization (of old habits), and reinterpretation (the coupling of old forms with new meanings) (Simpson 1973:89) are the cultural transformations most often revealed in the music and religion of African Americans.

There are still other processes at work in the act of cultural transformation. In my exploration of alterations in the Carriacou lineage code in chapter 2, I introduced a pattern of social transformation called reversal. When there is a social inversion in the agent or ownership of an element, though the mode, design, and function of the structure remain the same, one may classify it as a reversal. Reversal, then, may be applied to the turn in lineage construction, as in the case of the Cromanti, where the matrilineal system of the group switches and reverses itself to patrilineality. To see the process solely as a tactic of accommodation is to ignore the social traces still preserved in the system. Naming African gods with secondary European nominations represents another maneuver that absorbs without releasing the old. In this scheme Sango, for example, the African god of thunder and lightning, is conceived of as the powerful Christian saint, St. John.

But more than syncretizations and metaphorical transformations occur when Catholics worship alternately as Spiritual Baptists or when Anglicans present themselves as children of Orisa. The integrations have generated a continuum in all sects, with multiple layers of distant song practices superimposed within their services. The many forms of worship that include Sango

Baptists and African Baptists may lodge them upon various points upon a continuum between the Spiritual Baptist and Orisa religions.

Furthermore, the absorption of Indian, British, North American and Chinese traditions are indicated by Indian *lota* plates, flowers, perfumes, oils, and the bell, which are placed together around the mystic center pole of the Spiritual Baptist church. The international music, too, as generated from "mystical inspiration," "connaissance," and "spiritual travel," is an amalgam, and, like the translations of an Esu, is explicit but ironic, clear but filled with ambiguity and chance. The acculturative process in this enigmatic formula goes beyond that of the syncretism, borrowing, reinterpretation, or even the reversal of structural elements. Seemingly, contradictory elements coexist, reflecting a broad cultural ideology of double-voicedness—a religious double-voicedness.

Since the development of the literary theory put forth by Henry Louis Gates, Esu has become a leading figure and a culture marker in the analysis of African cultural forms. Gates's book *The Signifying Monkey* proposes the significance of ritual/language and contends that the Esu personality embodies an ideal that carries within it an artistic frame and performance style that infuses other endeavors and behaviors in the diaspora. The link between ancient ritual language and modern music and dance may be stretched to create a huge cultural necklace, a unified strand of linked artistic expressions. Gates's notion of this cultural chain couples the trickster figure of Yoruba religion to the signifying monkey of African-American oral literature, stacks oral ritual narratives upon the literary tradition of black writers, and conjoins ritual music with African-American blues, jazz, and rap. The mythical connection between the monkey and Esu remains conjectural, and the evidence linking the two crystallizes from linguistic interpretations of ritual poetry, myth, and practice (Gates 1988:15).

The monkey accompanied Esu on his passage to Cuba, but the monkey survives as a single entity celebrated in the signifying monkey tales. Esu disappeared in North American culture except for his ritual duties within the Louisiana Voodoo, but with the passing of Voodoo, it is believed, "the gods of Africa died" (Raboteau 1978:86).

The multiple-named figure is known in Nigeria as Esu Elegbara, in Benin (Dahomey) and Suriname as Legba, in Haiti as Papa Legba, in Cuba as Echu Elegua, in Brazil as Exu, and, when Voodoo was alive in Louisiana as PaPa LaBas. A single spirit may generate, through his/her function, other powers and, just so, in the Haitian family of spirits Legba spawned several related *loa* with specific roles. He works through his family as guardian of the highway (Legba Grand Chemin), ruler of the crossroads (Legba Kalfu), overseer of the household (Legba Mait' 'Bitation), and as the most important guardian of the gateway, crossroads, and highway (Attibon Legba) (Courlander 1960:320). In St. Lucia he is called Akeshew and in Trinidad his negative side was known as Shigidi (Schugudu) (Warner-Lewis 1978:22). Visualized in Yoruba iconography with two mouths and as dark, small, having a conical head, and always with a large phallus, the god of fecundity, Esu has penetrating eyes like fire coals. One of his legs is shorter than the other, "for one foot rests in the realm of the gods while the other is in the human world" (Gates 1988:6). Sexually ambiguous, his persona is overall rich with duality.

He is a trickster and the mediator between the divine and the earthly. As gatekeeper who opens the other world to humans, the guardian of the crossroads grants travel and communication. He is the interpreter who speaks the languages of divinities. In his absence the ritual texts are uninterpretable, the gods inaccessible, and the gates to the divine close. In the song-invocations below, collected from several sources, the Legba figures are addressed by name; and in the first song Legba Aguator is asked to reveal his nation. The responding voice replies in first person that he is a Nago (Yoruba) loa. *Ago*, a common expression in the Vodun songs, means "pay heed" or "listen" (Seabrook 1929:291).

Legba Aguator [Vodun Nago song]

Legba 'Guato'é!
Oh qui loa ou yé?
Ago loa 'm na!
Legba 'Guato'é!
Oh, qui loa ou yé là
Quitti quitt'yé
Oh Nèg' Nago loa 'm nà!
Legba 'Guato' é!
Qui loa ou yé? (Courlander 1960:296)

Legba Aguator e!
Oh what loa are you?
Ago I am a loa!
Legba Aguator e!

Oh what loa are you here?
Quitti quitt'ye,
Oh, I am a Nago loa!
Legba Aguator e! What loa are you? (Courlander 1960:345)

Legba [Vodun song]

Papa Legba
Ouvri barrier po' moin
Ago ye
Azima Legba
Ouvri barrier po' moin
Ouvri barrier po' moin
Ago ye — e (Herskovits 1936:705)

Atibon Legba [Vodun song]
Atibó Legba, l'uvri bayè pou mwê
Papa-Legba, l'uvri bayè pou mwê
Pou mwê pasé
Lo m'a tunê, m' salié loa-yo
Vodu Legba, l'uvri bayè pu mwê
Pu mwê sa râtré
Lo m'a tune, m'a rémesyè loa-yo Abobo

Atibo-Legba, remove the barrier for me, agoé
Papa Legba, remove the barrier
So I may pass through,
When I come back I will salute the *loa*
Voodoo Legba, remove the barrier for me,
So that I may come back;
When I come back, I will thank the *loa*, Abobo (Métraux 1972:101)

Legba [Vodun song]

Legba! soleil te leve, Legba
Ouvri barrie pou mon, Legba
Ouvri barrie pou toute moune yo
Mait' passe toute moune moin Bon Dieu . . .

Oui, Papa Legba, écoute gros mambo
Écoute houngan lui pou pauv' neg's 'Nan Guinée
Ouvri barrié pou entré, prie la vie nou donné
Fini soucis nou

Legba, the sun has risen
Open the door for me, Legba
Open the barrier for all
Let the good god enter
Yes, Papa Legba, listen to what the great mambo said
Listen to the houngan's petition for all the poor from Guinee
Open the gates so that we may enter and pray
That life will send us an end to our troubles . . . (Dunham 1994:129)

Sometimes a mound of clay erected outside of a Nigerian or Trinidadian shrine represents Esu, but in *Praisesong for the Widow* Paule Marshall humanizes Esu Elegba in the mirrored characterization of the old man Lebert. He sings and dances a Juba to display the ancient codes of Carriacou and introduce a new world, or rather, the old world, to the novel's central character, Avey. I have plucked out several descriptive phrases from various sections of the narrative and united them here to fully describe Elegba:

A stoop-shouldered old man with one leg shorter than the other limped from behind the screen. . . . He was dressed in a tieless long-sleeved white shirt frayed at the collars and cuffs and a pair of shapeless black pants without a belt. . . . His slight, winnowed frame scarcely seemed able to support the clothes he had on. He was close to ninety perhaps, his eyes as shadowed as the light in the rum shop and the lines etched over his face like the scarification marks of a thousand tribes . . . [with a] gaze that called to mind a jeweler's loupe or a laser beam in its ability to penetrate. . . . 'We di la wen Juba . . .' he sang,[6] and his voice also sounded more youthful. Moreover, it had taken on a noticeably feminine tone. The same was true of his gestures. The hand snapping the invisible skirt back and forth, the thrusting shoulders, the elbow flicking out—all were movements of a woman. (Marshall 1983: 160–61, 179, 250)

The gender ambiguity of the character is explicit through his feminine mime of the Juba dance. In the Carriacou Juba, two women imitate the movements of the other, suggesting the mirrored duplicity imaged by Esu.

Gates, too, illuminates the complex essence of Esu and proposes the reflection of his properties in the character of African-American literature and musical culture. Taking the physique and function of Esu as symbol, Gates determines the individual attributes to represent satire, parody, irony, magic, indeterminacy, uncertainty, open-endedness, chance, ambiguity, sexuality, disruption, reconciliation, betrayal and loyalty, closure and disclosure, encasement and rupture (Gates 1988:6). These are qualities also found in the North American Signifying Monkey tales. If broadly interpreted, one may extend these properties as the musical intentions of the blues, jazz, and other improvised African-American and Caribbean musical genres.

Gates uses the term *Signifyin(g)* to denote the African-American rhetorical device of metaphoric speech, a speech of innuendo, a language of trickery. It is making fun of a person, doing battle with a person, controlling, manipulating, reducing a person through insult, shaming, lying, challenge (dirty dozens, rap, toast), calling names, paying homage, teaching and elevating. We attribute each of these Signifyin(g) attitudes to those in West African music whether intended by the composer or delivered by the performer, audience response, or context.

The hypothesis underpinning the theory of Signifyin(g) represents Esu's personality as a multifaceted cultural idiom, thereby creating out of rituals, myth, and literature a bold critical method. It offers interpreters of diasporic music an open path toward theoretical formulations and enlivens the assumptions that ritual survivals proclaim: the intrinsic relationship between language and music, the cultural base of musical meaning, the specialized coding of African musical aesthetics. The theory opens the exploration of the "Africanness" of rap music not merely in its structural principles but in its function and meaning; it revives and encourages the now outdated structuralist tracing, for instance, of coincidences in African gesture and dance movements. The theoretical principles in *The Signifying Monkey* cushion and bring logic to the unexplainable in Caribbean culture. For example, they help to expound the very difficult logic behind the double-voiced union of Sango and St. John. It justifies a religious dual membership that seems to violate the basic concepts of Christian religious belief which some interpret as incompatible and valorizes for us the simultaneous adherences that appear to adherents as natural expressions of loyalty to mixed cultural streams. The very development of Creole languages may be explained through the Esu figure, which projects the definition of "creole" through his double-mouthedness, which symbolically manifests more than interpretation and translation, but a creatively absorbent retention of the antecedent languages of Europe and Africa.

The literary theory encourages my etymological search of the Big Drum song texts to identify not only ancestral names and attenuated meanings but also stylistic ingredients that reverse and thicken meaning, that infuse the music with mystical and magical intent.

Because members of the Yoruba nation were neither included in the original enslaved population nor brought as nineteenth-century indentured immigrants to Carriacou, significant cultural figures like Esu do not perform crucially in the Big Drum ritual. Even so, among the nations that make up the Carriacou ritual, there are hints of shared cultural inheritances. For example, the notion of cardinal directionality is found not only in Yoruba cosmology but also in Kongo thought (Thompson 1984:108) and Arada ideology (Carr 1953). The Igbos were not alone in desiring death over slavery; Kongo people, too, indulged in the final act of rebellion (Bilby 1983). Nor were the Yorubas and the Fon the only groups with a trickster figure. Anancy, the trickster spider of Akan provenance, though operating outside of the ritual and institutional domains (Pelton 1989:61), is perceived in every corner of the social space and spiritual arena as well.

Even though Anancy and Esu Elegbara are not formally a part of the Big Drum, principles associated with their personae permeate the event. The Legba invocation (perhaps from the Carriacou-Arada influence) may have influenced the program of the Big Drum as well. The placement of the three introductory songs bear reasoning analogous to the fleeting invitation of Esu in the larger rituals. Those songs resound like the Legba invocation in the Rada community of Trinidad, where three drum movements, unaccompanied by singing or dancing, invoke the spirit three times (Carr 1953). Before the commencement of the Big Drum, three Gwa Bélè songs, or short segments of each song—"Madame Philip-o," "Captain Desbat," and "Sandy Island"—are heard. They are songs from the Creole group, casually called "warm-up" tunes by the people, that lack the spiritual texts of the Nation songs. However, their performance takes on the formality of a staged concert, projecting a deeper function than that given by my friends in Carriacou. The introductory songs, I suggest, are ameliorative incantations originally designed to erase hostilities among the guests or to prepare them in some way for the rites that follow.

The grouping and positioning of these songs in the ritual may come from their symbolic references to conflict. The introductory songs include (1) an oral record of the sinking of a boat near the rock-island Kick'em Jenny; (2) an assertion of personal deception; and (3) an ancient fragmented account of a gun battle near the narrow, palmed island Sandy. The rock-island between Grenada and Carriacou, Kick'em Jenny is situated at the point where opposing currents clash, where the water becomes turbulent, suggesting the hostility in nature.[7] The songs are unified by the theme of conflict, representing parables of human struggle—not only with nature but the hostile rejection of individuals and the physical aggression of a military force.

Madame Philip-o [Gwa Bélè]

Madame Philip-o
Pu raison mwê
Jida la e bawé mwê

Jida la bawé mwê
Hypocrite bawé mwê
Jida bawé mwê
Madame Philip-o
Pu raison mwê

Madame Philip
In order to restrain me
Judas hinders me

Judas hinders me
The hypocrite rejects me
Judas denies me
Madame Philip-o
To restrain me

Captain Desbat [Gwa Bélè]

Captain Desbat, ai-o
U ba tan Venja kulé

U ba tan Venja néyé
Venja kulé bai Kick'em Jenny-o

Captain Desbat
Didn't you hear that the Avenger sank
Didn't you hear that the Avenger went under
The Avenger sank near Kick'em Jenny

Sandy Island [Gwa Bélè]
Mwê sorti Sandy Island, mama
Kanu ka ti way amba la
Kanu ka ti way amba la
Moka allé Sandy Island

I am leaving Sandy Island, mama
Guns shoot down there
Guns shoot down there
I am going to Sandy Island

After the triple-song prelude, the ancient repertoire begins with the Cromanti songs. As each dancer takes a singular turn in the ring, she or he enters an expressive arena in which to develop a mood, recall the past, and revive an identity. The moment of dance reigns as a gift to the person with a cause to argue, an illness to salve, or a memory to enact. It is in this individualistic way that alienated Africans begged for atonement, arched their laments, wailed their disappointments, taught ethical positions, laid the perpetrator open, and embarrassed the antisocial person. The texts guide us with their complex, ambiguous, metaphoric plays; parody and satire accompany the open-ended, improvised dances of chance, of uncertainty, adding excitement and strength to dance, funneling the absorption of spirits, filling the moment with more than dance. In the frank physicality of the dance, the image of Esu Elegbara permeates the spiritual as well as the social domains of the ring, and it is through the metaphor of Esu that dance enables the transcendence of the physical sea barrier as well as the mental partition separating the two worlds.

Exuberant rhythms entrain the dancers' movements, and the crowd joins in the imagery of flight. In the same way that the nation rhythms emblematize distant ethnic connections and call ancestors to the Big Drum, the Orisa and

Vodun rhythms signal flying gods to soar westward. And moving in the other direction, toward eastern spheres, the wanderings of the Spiritual Baptists are directed by the 'doption modes just as Rastafarian religious and political repatriation is made buoyant through drumming. In the mental travels hosted by rhythm, an enlightened baptism inspires the connaissance, the fascination with homeland, the revival of ancestral connectedness. I suggest that the Signifyin(g) beats, operating as codes that open the barriers and signal the divine, serve as rhythmic banisters that guide travel into private realms of spiritual imagination.

Four

Beg Pardon

Mené mwe conté-o
Mené mwe conté-o
Si mwe merité, pini mwe
Si mwe ba merité, padoné mwe

Help me to declare this
Help me to declare this
If I deserve it, punish me
If I don't deserve it, pardon me

—Big Drum Bongo

The act of composition in the Big Drum, like the social formulations in Carriacouan thought, reflects several cultural idioms syncretized during almost two centuries of performance. As I have suggested in the use of a
single myth to interpret ritual, survivals often exist in hidden levels of meaning
in music. The characteristics that I interpret first are the obvious structural
survivals; following that, I suggest cultural markers as influential on musical

structure. The age of the Big Drum songs, and their textual and compositional codes as well as the relationship to those of the Trinidad calypso, are hypothesized in this chapter.

It is clear that the structural content of the Nation songs may be traced to African origins, with their call-and-response patterning, voice and drum instrumentation, cyclephonic texture, reiterative statements, and integral association with dance. These elements are broadly termed "African"; no single stylistic factor can be drawn to establish the exact ethnic musical convention in the songs or to link them to specific musical cultures. Like the creolization in linguistic and social domains, the musical integration lessened stylistic differences to create a blended medium. Skips of thirds, fourths, and fifths as well as a step-wise motion are common in all Nation songs. The vocal range of the Nation songs is most often a sixth; the largest span, a tenth, is found in two Kongo songs. Although I sense in the Manding repertoire a characteristic triadic and melismatic movement, the sampling of songs is too small to conjecture an inheritance from a specific Mandingo repertoire. Indeed, in most types the small number of songs precludes the construction of a specific model for each nation type. Therefore, I avoid affirming specific musical origins from source repertoires.

A single West African group may own hundreds of repertoires and essential rhythms. Therefore the possibility of uncovering the source musics or characteristic rhythms of each Caribbean nation is bleak. What is more important, however, is knowing how the people used music as a code for ethnic designation. Through this we are able to formulate, to some extent, the social desires of the people.

In Africa the responsorial form exists in six basic types, as outlined by Nketia (1974:141). Other more involved forms occur in multi-part African choral traditions in which canon, hocket, ostinato, and instrumental music are employed (145). The call-and-response patterns summarized in table 5 are all found in the Big Drum repertoire.

Like formal structure, the question of texture must also be examined. Multi-part singing is frequent in African genres. It is widely reported in Akan music, as in the following anonymous excerpt dated 1797. It reads: "The Cromantines far excel the others in music, whose tunes are sung in canto fermo; while the Cormantines perform their airs in different parts not unlike our glees" (Abrahams and Szwed 1983:293).

Table 5. Big Drum call-and-response patterns

Leader	Chorus
1. Single repeated phrase (a)	+ exact repeated imitation (a) = a a^1 a a^2
2. Single repeated phrase (a)	+ repeated response (b) = a b a b
3. Two alternate phrases (a, c)	+ repeated responses (b) = a b c b
4. Two alternate phrases (a, c)	+ two alternate phrases (b, d) = a b c d
5. Alternations followed by a combined leader-chorus conclusion	
6. Use of an introductory section	

The Asanti song below, transcribed by the nineteenth-century chronicler Edward Bowdich, illustrates the use of parallel thirds and also the short repeated phrase-answer. It is a song combining the second type in table 5 (unchanging response) and the fifth type (combined leader-chorus at conclusion). Bowdich notes quite innocently that the Christmas song, sung by one man and one woman or more, has a surprising regularity, "and its transition from G major to C major is very harmonious (Bowdich 1819:368). He points to a major essence in the repertoire in discussion here in which such "transitions" allow the tunes' continuous restatement and avoids harmonic finality.

Contrary to the great volume of African vocal music, in which the practice of overlapping phrases occurs, the monophonic song lines of the contempo-

12. Accra fetish hymn (Thomas Edward Bowdich). Special Collections, University of Delaware, Newark.

rary Big Drum do not cross, converge, or break into heterophony, nor does the ancient and stylized practice of parallel intervalic singing occur. The lack of these traits (linear overlapping, heterophony, and parallel intervalic singing) in the modern performance produces a peculiarly strict monophony that indicates this music has other influences. In the 1956 Pearse recording of old head singers, however, there are a few instances where the practice of overlapping does appear.

All other vocal traditions of modern Carriacou implement harmonic treatments as well as heterophonic textures. The historic *cantiques*, previously sung at wakes and prayer meetings, were usually performed in a fragmented part harmony—remnants of French hymnody. Besides this, the nineteenth-century Sankey hymn, as used in the Spiritual Baptist service, is inventively reharmonized and orchestrated with textless vocalizations. Improvised prayer/chants are freely heterophonic and often sung above a traditional hymn tune, creating an improvised, polyphonic, vocal chorale prelude. And, more than this, the *parang* songs, composed and sung by parading troops of musicians during the Christmas season, often involve harmonized choral and string instrumental settings. In the same way, both the string band music of Windward village and the Quadrille of L'Esterre project melodic lines rooted in harmonic principles.

Despite the harmonic practices of genres surrounding the Big Drum, the texture of the ritual music continues seemingly untouched. I attribute the strict monophony of the Big Drum to a self-conscious handling of the ancient tunes engendered through a respect for the age of the genre and a conscious desire to retain musical aspects thought to be African. This musical behavior may be inherited from aesthetic notions in historical practice. We note a convention that limits musical creation to text formulation that also reveals a respect for and protective attitude toward the repertoire. My aged culture bearer Pofella Corion expressed to me the attitude toward composition reflected by the value placed upon the treasured collection in this way: "You can make a song for yourself; that song no natural, you want to know the old time natural song" (Corion 1983). But, more meaningfully, it is known that ancestors, critical of changing musical tastes, respond only to music performed within the strict codes of their own music-making. Therefore, to reach the ancestors musically, melodies must realize ancient performance practices.

In many Nation songs a short, persistent leader/chorus interplay projects

13. Quadrille band led by Canute Caliste, violinist.

the short, reiterative call-and-response paradigm illustrated in this double-phrase Kongo song "Kongo Malabu":

Kongo Malabu [Kongo]

Kongo Malabu
Pei Kongo

Kongo earth
My country, Kongo

Kon - go Ma - la - bu   Pei   Kon - go

A structure comparable to that of "Kongo Malabu" dominates several Kalendas and Bongos that are, like the Nation songs, survivals from ancient African dance/songs. But, unexpectedly, an analogous short-phrase call-and-response appears in many turn-of-the-century items. I suggest that these late texts were set upon ancient, revised melodies. The short, persistent chorus answer, common in the Nation songs, is found in five Frivolous songs. An example of this is a Cheerup of the second type of call-and-response (see table 5), in which the leader phrases alternate and the chorus phrases remain invariable.

Popo ave Orelia [Cheerup]

Popo ave Orelia
Ka bulé engine Belmont

Popo sa ki tombé
Ka bulé engine Belmont

Popo and Orelia
They burn down Belmont's engine

Popo falls down
They burn down Belmont's engine

Po - po   avé O - re - lia   Ka   bu - lé en - gine Bel- mont

I discussed the cyclic expositional structure of the repertory in the introduction, and because of the essential nature of this element I wish to complete the analysis here with a transcription of "Ena-o" set upon a cyclephonic score to explain the density and musical interplay more thoroughly than is possible through linear scoring or verbal analysis. Figure 14 illuminates the cyclic interrelationships that produce an undulating harmonic concord.

Composition in the Big Drum

The vocal extemporization that chantwell Lucian Duncan calls "composition" centers primarily upon the alteration of texts. A practice most likely more extensively employed by previous generations of chantwell/composers, it creates minor melodic and rhythmic transmutations. An example of an improvised type of leader-statement survives in the next song, "Iama Diama."

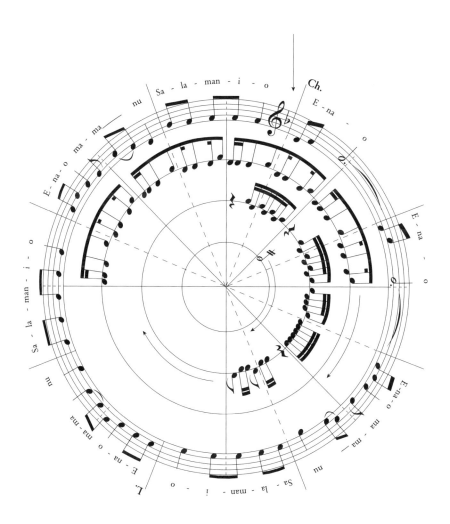

14. Cyclephonic full score.

The solo phrases are interchangeable and, as in "An Accra Fetish Hymn," the words influence the creation of melodic variations.

Iama Diama [Igbo]

Chorus: Iama Diama, Igbo Lélé, Iama
Leader: I'm a polin Igbo
Chorus: Iama Diama, Igbo Lélé, Iama
Leader: Mwe polin Igbo
Chorus: Iama Diama, Igbo Lélé, Iama
Leader: Ayen ba ka fé Igbo

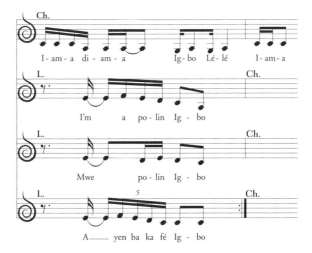

The concept of song composition permits the reuse of tunes, a recycling that serves to protect and prolong the life of melodies while introducing immediate and relevant textual materials. In the early years great events were encapsulated in texts and superimposed upon the treasured musical legacy. With this unspoken compositional theory, the life of an ancient melody is ensured and protected from extreme alteration. The term *composition* as used by Big Drum practitioners actually applies to the act of song leading, which includes extemporization on the song during performance. The interpolation or omission of a single phrase such as "firelight," "kachimbo," "deliso," and "ai, mama" may alter the impetus and rhythm of the song.

Illuminating the Carriacou compositional ideal and its reliance on revision, Eileen Southern's research on North American folk and spiritual songs clarifies choices of the composer in African-type composition. She states that "Consciously or unconsciously, he [she] may (1) improvise on a song already in existence; (2) combine material from several old songs to make the new one; or (3) compose the song entirely from new materials." Southern points to the first choice as the favorite (Southern 1997:185).

Spontaneous composition in the Big Drum occurred most often as an emotional response to tragedy, undertaken as a consolation of grief or alienation, as a vindictive action of derision against an enemy, as a vindication of innocence, or as a weapon in the threat of litigation. Composed by Lucian Duncan after the arrest of her friend's son, the Hallecord "Police Lawen" is a rare instance of composition after 1920. While the mother, Lucian, and the community kept vigil at the police station in support of the incarcerated young man, the song took shape. As Ms. Duncan formed the new Hallecord, the community joined in at the response. The voice of the song is that of the young man.

Police Lawen [Hallecord]
Chorus: Wegima mwe semblé
Wegima mwe semblé-o
Police lawen pu pwa mwe
Leader: Police lawen pu pwa mwe
Mie police lawen deyé mwe

Chorus: My family is here
My family is here
The police imprison me
Leader: The police imprison me
They witness the queen's police surround me

We-gi-ma mwe sem-blé - o We-gi-ma mwe sem - blé-o   po-lice deyé-o pu pwa mwe

Po - lice   la - wen pu pwa mwe mi - é   pwa po-lice la - wen de - yé   mwe

I present below a transcription of an interview with Lucian Duncan in which she describes the circumstances surrounding her first composition, a Kalenda. Upon the complaint of her ailing uncle, a musician whose hand had been injured in an attack by a donkey, she, at thirteen years of age, "made a song for herself."

Q. What else have you composed?

A. This one I tell you [the Hallecord above] and Kalenda. One time me uncle has a donkey and it was bad. Well, he see the donkey go and fight with another one. He try see if he could part them. He go holding to drag it out. As he go to hold the donkey, he fling him out. The donkey take he hand. If people didn't they dey near, the donkey would a take he hand till he bite it to the bone. Spend about a month in Carriacou hospital and in Grenada hospital. We go to carnival. He used to dance this kalenda. He used to beat drum as well. He stand there, he start to cry. He say, "Look at me *compere* [kin], me compere Duncan! Drum beating—I can't beat and I want to dance, me hand *hambuging* [annoying] me." I stand up and say: [she sings] "Today, today" [she begins to cry] Any time I remember to sing this . . . When I sing that song . . . I remember him. He say, "Look at me standing here and drum beating and I can't beat, can't dance. Compere Duncan!" (My father was Ajian Duncan. Anto, Cyrus all were great drummer. All drummers. That's why you see all the children want to beat the drum.)

[She sings] Under the mango tree in Arima
Today, today
Today, today in Arima
Today, today
Elie boy donkey bite your poor hand
Today, today
Nobody know your grievant
Today, today
Today, today in Aruba
Elie boy donkey bite your poor hand
Today, today nobody don't know you worries
Today, today me uncle stand up and he can't beat

Oh, God, the drum stop, man. They had to stop the drum.

Q. Did you make it up on the spot?

A. Right where me stand up. I went crying and he went calling. "Where is Elie?" Elie was in Aruba at the time. "Look at me hand. I can't make a note with me hand." And it was the right hand.

Extended Forms

More than any other type, the Bélè exemplifies the more obvious syncretism of African and European musical models. Longer phrases than those found in the Nation songs, melodic sequencing, and triadic Western harmonic implications govern this song type.

As the melodic phrase lengthens, so does the overall formal structure of the Bélè reorganize itself. This is dramatically shown in the incipient dance form the *Dama*, which may have grown from the Bélè (Pearse 1956:6). The song "Dama" survives as the single example of the verse-chorus song.

Dama [Dama]

Verse: Dépi tâ Gawé alé oh
Dépi tâ Gawé mowi
Dépi tâ Gawé kité, Mama
Se li ka di "Bô ju" Madam
Chorus: Dama, ai Dama
Dama, ai Dama
Dama, ai Dama
Sé bel pézi pu wè Dama

Verse: Ever since Garraway went away
Ever since Garraway died
Ever since Garraway left
It is he (or she) who is saying "Good morning, Madam"
Chorus: Dama, ai Dama
Dama, ai Dama
Dama, ai Dama
What a pleasure it is to see the Dama (Pearse 1956:6)

The Bélè Kawé "Lawen Dama-o" includes rhythmically coherent motives in the first three measures that dramatically transmute themselves to a lively, syncopated rhythmic pattern in the last phrase. The minor melody closes on the dominant tone, which propels the melody into continuous repetitions. A clear Western harmonic progression is outlined in the melody of this song.

The call-and-response structure controls this lyrical piece in a very different way from the short, repetitious responses common to the Nation songs. The response phrases elongate the melodic flow rather than forming a contrasting melody. The design of the phrases does not differentiate the lead call from the chorus answer, and because of this the song is formed as a single, coherent melodic line that could be convincingly sung by a single voice rather than by leader and chorus. Other than the syncopated pattern at the closure of the piece, the song melody does not reveal an African style.

"Lawen Dama-o" is a favorite in the modern repertoire, but only one verse of the multi-verse setting is sung today. I have collected several strophes from various sources. The scattered survival of the song suggests to me that other items may also at one time have been similarly richly endowed with verses. The song text is filled with inscrutable images of the now deserted cliff village, Lance la Roche, of nature and a haunted relationship.

Lawen Dama-o [Bélè Kawé]

Chorus: Lawen Dama-o
Pa di mwe sa-o
Chantwell: Pa di mwe sa-o
Pa di mwe sa Lawen Dama-o

Lawen Dama-o
Pa di mwe sa-o
Mokai na Lance La Roche
Conté raison bai Mama

Lawen Dama-o
Pa di mwe sa-o
La plui tombé-o
Solie couché in Lance La Roche

Lawen Dama-o
Pa di mwe sa-o
La plui tombé-o
Tonné wulé in Lance La Roche

Lawen Dama-o
Pa di mwe sa-o
La plui tombé
Hélé nom mwe na wegima

Chorus: Queen Dama
Don't tell me that
Chantwell: Don't tell me that
Queen Dama
Don't tell me that

Queen Dama
Don't tell me that
I will go to Lance La Roche
To tell my side of the story to Mama

Queen Dama
Don't tell me that
Rain continues to fall
And the sun sets in Lance La Roche

Queen Dama
Don't tell me that
Rain falls
And thunder rolls in Lance La Roche

Queen Dama
Don't tell me that
Rain falls
My name resounds among my people

Word endings are significantly placed in most songs where names, especially, are fixed with a vowel or the final vowel is elongated with an "e" or "o" or an elision of the two. In "Lawen Dama-o" old head singers underline the elongation of endings as significant and essential to the style (McDaniel 1985:187). Name alterations of "o," "e," or "oi" as final vowels permeate the Big Drum repertoire just as daily long-distance salutations prolong the neighborly shout in musical ways.[1]

Name shouting is a part of the historical practice of the death announcement called "running the news." Death was until recently heralded in Patois by young men who rode throughout the villages crying: "Sa ki tan parlé lot. I kai tewé kat demi, merci Bunjé. Sesé Jeannette Philip mort." Now they announce the news in English: "All who hear tell others. She will be buried tomorrow at four-thirty, please God. Sister Jeannette Philip is dead."

The age-old custom of the death announcement (which frames the importance of names) entered the Hallecord song group. Of my sample of seventeen Hallecords, seven mourn the death of a family member. In "Na Goli-o" the death of a brother is announced and the singer questions: "Mes ami u ba tan lankan Garden fwé mwe ka hélé?" ("Friends, don't you hear the wail of my brother Garden's name?"). In a second Hallecord, "Sesé Ani-o," the text states that Ani's name is *wulé*, meaning "ringing" or being "broadcast," for her mother has died. Both songs follow.

Na Goli-o [Hallecord]

Na Goli-o, Maté
Hélé-o
Na Goli-o, Maté
Mes amis u ba tan Garden ka hélé
Mwe couché la su kabann mwe ka dodo
Mes ami u ba tan lankan fwé mwe ka hélé
Na Goli-o, Maté,
Hélé-o
Na Goli-o, Maté
Mes amis u ba tan Garden ka hélé

In Goli, Maté
Cry out!

In Goli, Mate
My friends, don't you hear Garden's name called out?
As I lie in bed, asleep
My friends, don't you hear my brother's name called out?
In Goli, Mate
Wail!
In Goli, Mate
My friends, do you not hear Garden's name hailed out?

Sesé Ani-o [Hallecord]

Sesé Ani-o, levé-o
Sesé Ani-o, levé-o
Ani-o, no u ka wulé
Ani-o no u ka wulé
Ai, Ani Mama lamo

Sister Ani, get up!
Sister Ani, get up!
Ani, your name is "ringing"
Ani, your name is "ringing"
Oh, Ani, your mother has died

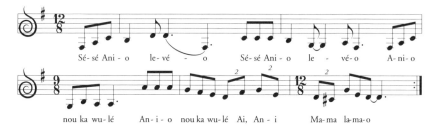

Sé- sé Ani - o   le- vé   -   o   Sé- sé Ani - o   le   -   vé- o   A- ni - o

nou ka wu- lé   An- i - o   nou ka wu- lé   Ai, An - i   Ma- ma la-ma-o

Although the melodic coincidence between "Na Goli-o" and "Sesé Ani-o" is multiple, "Na Goli-o" is considered an independent song and not a variant of "Sesé Ani-o." New melodies were not fully accepted as Big Drum material; new texts, however, were called new compositions exactly as chantwell-lyricists were regarded as "composers."

Because the Big Drum concept of song lies in the text rather than in the melody, many tunes, especially of the Hallecord set, bear a relatedness. Note the melodic similarity in the content of the two songs above—the coincidences in their diminished chord outlining, the octave skip, and the closure on the fifth.

I sense that many Hallecords stem from a single Hallecord that spawned the others. "Hélé, Mwe Pléwé" bears a melodic movement in the first phrase that is imitated in many other Hallecords. Because the octave leap and lowered seventh step, common in many Hallecords, are absent from this song, I propose this item as the antecedent form of the later Hallecords.

Hélé, Mwe Pléwé [Hallecord]

Hélé, mwe pléwé
Lamò sala bulé
Lamò Mama mwe ka pli bulé

Listen to my cry, I am weeping
The death of that one burns
But my mother's death burns more (Pearse 1956:6)

Plé- wé mwe plé- wé   ai, la mort sa la bu - lé

Ai, la mort sa la bu- lé   tom- bo ma- ma mwe, mwe plé- wé

Like that in "Lawen Dama-o," the call-and-response pattern in the Halle-cord differs significantly from that in the Nation songs. The longer answer-phrase of the Hallecord functions almost like a refrain between the leader "verses" rather than as short-phrased interjections as in the older songs.

To distinguish further, unlike "Hélé, Mwe Pléwé," the mature Hallecord often commences with an introductory phrase in which a name is called. The name is the subject of the song, the site of the story's action, or, as in the next song, the name of the song's composer. Loancine, the subject and composer of the next song, intoned her own name at the beginning to summon Mastiod, a nephew, at the news of the death of his brother, Nevi.

Loancine was a healer, a doctor of folk medicine. Specializing in treating babies struck with *maljo* (*mal yeux*, "evil eye")[2] she was sought after by Carria-couans and people from surrounding islands when their bodies experienced a "broken" sensation in the limbs and an incapacitating stomach sickness—the effects of *maljo*. This illness most often attacked children, sometimes causing them suddenly to become limp and feeble. As a disabling negative energy, *maljo* may be transmitted through the gaze of a hostile and envious person. Testimonies of such attacks and the more serious witchcraft of *wanga, obeah,* and *kokoma* are scattered in the songs discussed later.

It was thought that the tragedy was orchestrated by jealous people who hired an obeahman to alter natural laws inducing Nevi Allert's death. The story, as told by Nevi's daughter, the late Zeea Allert, is that Nevi's enemies took a portion of rope from his boat, delivering it to the obeahman. The ob-eahman infused the rope with malevolent herbs and medicated potions that caused Nevi's boat, on a trip to Grenada, to capsize; the keel hit Nevi's head, killing him. The song:

Loancin-o [Hallecord]

Loancin-o, en allé
En allé, en allé, Mastiod
Nevi allé ba wivé
Nevi allé, ba wivé
Mama mwe
I allé L'Abbe
or: (I wivé Les Tantes)]
I ba wivé

Loancin-o, let us go
Let us go, let us go, Mastiod
Nevi went and won't return
Nevi went and won't return
Oh, Mama
He went to Grenville
or: (He reached Les Tantes islands)]
He won't return

Lo - an - cin - o   en   al - lé - (o)   en   al - lé,   en   al - lé

Mas- ti - od   Ne - vi   al - lé___   ba   wi - vé   Ne - vi___   al - lé   ba   wi - vé

ma - ma   mwe - o   en   l'Ab - bé   i   ba   wi - vé

Of the 129 songs known to me, only six omit naming a person or place. It is usually a first name like Ovid, Popo, Tim Bwai ("Boy"), or Antoine, but sometimes last names like Bedeau, Desbat, Cudjo, or Quashie are also found.

Carriacou continues to be a name-calling society that emphasizes the meanings behind names. Children assume descriptive "home" names that reflect their personality, family position, and the circumstances at their birth. Ende, Myoni ("My-own-I"), Gentle, Sugar, Pofella, and Welcome are familiar names expressing the sibling position as last child, the child's personality or the esteem held by the family. Kinship terms used as a form of respect include Mudder, Mama, Papa, Tantie, Sesé ("sister"), and Cousin. Other, older, titles absorbed into the songs include Captain, Mesir, and Lawen ("queen"). Culture bearers simply describe the practice of personal naming as "a bit of love."

In Akan societies people award names to children according to the day of their birth. Cudjo is assigned to the boy born on Monday, Kwabena born on Tuesday, Quaco on Wednesday, Quao on Thursday, Cuffee on Friday, Quamin on Saturday, and Quashie to the boy born on Sunday. For the female child, the following corresponding names are given: Juba, Beneba, Couba,

Abba, Phibba, Mima, and Quasheba (Abrahams and Szwed 1983:101). In North America, Surinam, Jamaica, and Carriacou, where significant populations of Akans live, Quamina, Cudjo, and Quashie survive as surnames. The cultural implications of the name in Akan society can not be overemphasized, for the systematic awarding of natal day-names operates within a complex scheme of naming that even connects concepts of reincarnation and cross-cousin marriage (Rattray 1927:80). Given the lack of personal choice during slavery, we do not know how the Cromanti were able to maintain African names over colonial names, but it may have been a result determined by their self-concept and exclusivity within slave society.

Stylistic Elements

Along with our focus on the structural elements, compositional intent, cultural ideation, vocal style, and timbre deserve consideration as major features in musical traditions. In the Big Drum, which is most often an outdoor event, the voice performs in tandem with aggressive, unmuted drumming. Despite the strength of the voices, the excited calls and laughter of the pleased audience may sometimes drown out the vocal dimension of the performance. In this setting the chantwell must project in an open, throaty, lower range. The chorus responses, placed at the unison or octave, are casually engaged in with singers offering little or more of their voices depending upon the enthusiasm for the song.

There is little sliding in the attack of tones, nor is there significant deviation from the diatonic scale system. With this and the very limited melisma in the songs, it may be said that they are delivered in a simplicity of style.

The male *chantuel* is a rarity today, but an especially evocative male vocal stylization can be heard in the Chamba song, "Ai-o, Kanjuri-o," on the 1956 Pearse recording. Although credits are not listed, the voice is that of master drummer Sugar Adams.

The vocal timbre of the two functioning groups on Carriacou differs greatly, and the quality heard on the Pearse and Lomax recordings deviates from these to an even greater degree. The dissimilarity seems to rest upon the generational eras of the three groups—the youngest group, the mature chorus, and the recorded voices of a past generation. The tri-generationality of the groups affords us examples of the gradual process in the loss of stylistic features.

The Pearse recording memorializes the sound of the old parents, and from this document students seek to revive early nuanced vocalizations. One of the singers on the album is Rachel John, an outstanding vocalist of a previous age. Her husky, dark timbre can be heard in the vocal projection of her grand-daughter, Estimie Andrews, who passes on the specific nuances in the delivery of word endings and Patois phrases.

The Textual Classification

The modes of Signifyin(g) may be extended beyond literature and applied also to music. As suggested by Gates, the extent of Signifyin(g) in jazz is over-whelming in its continuing process of repetition, revision, and reversal. In fact, improvisation, a revisionist art, is in itself a form of Signifyin(g) (Gates 1988:63). In addition to this, artists pay homage to one another by altering and rearranging the signature tunes of their musical ancestors, and, through this honorific act, create a place for themselves within a musical lineage.

Signifyin(g) is a rhetorical device steeped in metaphor and based upon rep-etition and revision. Its language names, elevates, tells tales, challenges, in-sults, and shames in ways consonant with the purpose of the Big Drum, which pays homage to the ancestors, keeps history, and makes fun of and controls the irreverent.

I isolate the texts of the Big Drum in eleven thematic groups: ancestor ven-eration, beg pardon, great event, picong (derision), satire, social control, la-ment, consolation, migration, wanga (mental war), and protest. These group-ings fit naturally into the characteristics of the Esu Elegba figure translated as Signifyin(g) metaphors. The song classification in table 6, is on the left, and the corresponding rhetorical act, translated into song behavior, on the right.

The complex issue in text interpretation, especially of ancient and foreign texts of the black diaspora, is knowing who is the signifier and who is signified upon. In songs in which the voice shifts, not only between chantwell and cho-rus but also within the statements of each, with the singer sometimes taking the role of the signified (see "Police Lawen"), it is difficult to ascertain if the singer is the subject of the song. Because the song owners are no longer the composers/performers of the songs, the social function has drifted, the mean-ings have been scrambled, and the force of signification has been diluted. There is no doubt that the early performers, profiting from contextual infor-

Table 6. Big Drum thematic groups and the intent of the songs in each

Thematic group	Song intent
Ancestor veneration	Paying homage
Beg Pardon	Petitioning
Great Event	"Lying," telling tales
Picong, Mespris, Fatigue	Teasing, insulting, making fun of, abusing
Satire	Controlling, manipulating
Social Control	Shaming, "schooling," naming
Lament	Paying homage
Consolation	Elevating
Migration	"Lying," telling tales
Wanga	Doing battle with a person
Protest	Challenging, boasting

mation and shared knowledge, sang these texts with relish, emphasizing double entendre and exploiting metaphors of indirection.

Wanga in Women's Songs

The term *wanga* (*ouanga*) appears in East and West African languages and also in Louisiana Creole culture and means "a spell or charm" (Turner 1969:43). I use it to classify songs (three Bélè Kawé, three Gwa Bélè, a single Igbo, a Kalenda, a Man Kalenda, and a Piké) of interpersonal animosity. The Bélè Kawé songs seem to portray aggression in social behavior best. Danced historically by women, the Bélè Kawé gets its name from the position in which the dancers' skirts are held—out to the sides of the dancer in a fashion that appears to imitate the stance of defense (*carré*) in stickfighting (Pearse 1956:4). In this instance, at least the name of the dance, if not the dance itself, reflects the meaning of many of its songs. Usually in other repertoires the song themes belie the affect in the dance. In the Hallecord, for instance, mournful texts accompany a dance considered "hot" and enticing. The Bélè texts reveal consternation at the betrayal of a friend and dismay at gossip with evil intent. Fear, competition, and jealousy project through the song language, indicating conflict with a personal enemy called the hypocrite, *lelmi* ("enemy"), *Jida* ("Judas"), and *jab* ("devil"). The themes of the Wanga songs of battle include implications of female competition for a mate, the social stigma associated with childlessness, and the controlling attitudes of reproach against the *slack* ("promiscuous"), the *reigner* ("loose"), the *jamette* ("low class"), and the "fast" woman.

I choose two of three songs with the title "Dandi" as examples. The first is the response of a childless woman to someone who has cursed her as barren. She explains that, if God would grant it, she would have a child. The second is sung by a leader of an association of women, whose members punish her with exclusion.

Dandi é Yé [Bélè Kawé]

Dandi é yé
Mwe ba tini ish-o
Dandi é yé
Si sa gaé ish-o
Papa ba bam mwe-o
Pu (mwe) hélé nom mwe na wegima

Dandi and you all!
I have no children
Dandi and you all!
If I could buy a child I would
God did not grant it to me
For me to shout my name among my kin

Dandi é yé Alle Mandé Jida [Bélè kawé]

Dandi é yé
Allé mandé Jida yé
Sa mwe fé yo
Dandi é yé
Dandi é yé
Allé mandé Jida yé
Sa mwe fé yé
Ai, Sésé, moka meté ka mwe na wejima mwe
Jida ba vlé ouè mwe

Jida hai mwe-o
Jida trahi mwe
Jida ba vlé ouè mwe

Dandi and you all!
Go and ask that Judas
What I have done to you all
Dandi and you all!
Dandi and you all!
Go and ask that Judas
What I have done to you all
Ai, Sister, when I am in the gang, I am leading
Judas won't see me
Judas hates me
Judas betrays me
Judas won't see me

The song "La U C'est" repeats the expression of conflict, "Jida," as well as references to methods of witchcraft that could be employed against an opponent—maljo, wanga, and obeah. The name *Dandi* is used again in this song as in all those above.

La U C'est [Gwa Bélè]
La u c'est laisse parlé
La u c'est laisse Jida parlé-o
La u c'est laisse passé, Dandi-o

Mama mwe ba ka ma obeah
Sésé mwe ba ka maé wanga-o
La u c'est laisse Jida passé, Dandi-o

Let them talk
Let the hypocrites talk
Ignore them, Dandi

Mama, I do not handle obeah
Sister, I don't do wanga
Ignore the Judas, Dandi

As a result of the confirmed patterns of migration, the population of Carriacou has been, since emancipation, predominantly female. Yet, families remained intact throughout the protracted periods of male absence. The next Wanga song indicates the exacting sphere of the yard, which symbolizes the private domain of the family and the spiritual space for memory. Visitors with unkind words are not welcome in the yard. The cultural view of the potency and power of words in adversarial contexts is succinctly expressed in the Carriacou proverb: "The tongue of a black person is like a whip" ("*Lang Neg c'est liane*").

Mwe Di No [Gwa Bélè]

Mwe di no-yo
Mwe di no-yo
Mwe ba vlé Jida sa la
Na laku mwe
Mwe ba vlé Jida sa la
Na laku mwe
Tini mauvais Jida amba lang

I say "no"!
I say "no"!
I don't want those hypocrites
In my yard
I don't want that Judas
In my yard
They have bad words under their tongues

Jida, Mwe ba vlé Jida [Woman Kalenda]

Ai, Jida, mwe ba vlé Jida
Jida mwe ba passé
Hélé-ai-o
Hélé-ai-o
Hélé-ai-o
Hélé-ai-o
Hélé-o-ai-o
Jida, mwe ba vlé Jida

Oh, Judas, I don't like a Judas
Judas won't leave me alone
Hele-ai-o
Hele-ai-o
Hele-ai-o
Hele-ai-o
Hele-o-i-o
Judas, I don't like a Judas

Tewé Wanga U Meté [Piké]

Tewé wanga la zo meté
Bam mwe
Tewé!
Tewé-o!
or: (Beau Sejour)

Take out the wanga
You put on me
Take it out!
Take it out!
or: (Beau Sejour!) [the name of a large plantation]

Songs of Migration and Protest

The failure of sugar, the withdrawal of the British land-owners, and unproductive farming due to ecological imbalance forced the newly emancipated people of Carriacou to create a cycle of migration. The routes of travel to Barbados, Trinidad, and Grenada emerged after emancipation and grew to form a cultural pattern. Trinidad, the initial and principal host country, offered free passage, a house, land for private use, and a wage for canefield work immediately after emancipation (Hill 1973:23). In the 1920s and 1930s, canal building in Panama; cobble street work, bridge building, and subway construction in New York; and, still later, the oil-refining industries in Aruba and Venezuela attracted migrating Carriacou workers. One may trace the regions of the shifting phases of migration through song, for the texts reveal the foreign place names.

Trinidad's later history was culturally variegated as a result of early political acts, especially when Spain had opened the borders of the underpopulated island to colonization in 1783. With the Cedula of Population, which offered free land grants, Spain welcomed Catholics from any country. The policy continued after the British invasion and capture of the island in 1797. By the turn of the nineteenth century Trinidad was the home of immigrants from the surrounding French colonies whose lives had been recently disrupted by revolution, by the threat of revolution, or by the hostility experienced by French subjects on other islands ceded to Britain. In a short time, therefore, England found that it governed a French- and Patois-speaking nation.

Carriacouans shared their songs wherever they traveled. They took Carriacou musical culture with them, and it became a part of the plurality of song styles in the multifariously musical island of Trinidad (Hill 1973:44). They also borrowed songs, like the popular Bongo item below, which was appropriated by Carriacouans from their Trinidad sojourn. It is one of the set of protest songs sung as political reaction to the suppression by the British government of Patois speech in the schools and of the Bongo dance.

In My Own Native Land [Man Bongo]

In my own, in my own-o
In my own native land
In my own, in my own-o
In my own native land
Pa sa bongo com mwe vlé
or: (Pa sa parlé com mwe vlé)
or: (Pa sa dubout com mwe vlé)
In my own native land

In my own, in my own-o
In my own native land
In my own, in my own-o
In my own native land
I can't bongo as I please
or: (I can't speak as I please)
or: (I can't stand up as I please)
In my own native land

The next protest song falls outside the usual boundaries of Big Drum vocabulary, tone, and sentiment in its conscious effort to teach and inspire self-respect and unity among migrants.

Le Ouè Mwe La [Juba]

Noé, ai, Noé
Noé, ai, Noé
Jens di tampon
Le ouè mwe la
Le ouè mwe ba la
Supporté respec pu jens mwe

Gal la-e yé sorti Babado
Gal la-e yé sorti Ginado
Le ouè mwe la
Le ouè mwe ba la
Supporté respec pu jens mwe

Black people!
Black people!
Black people tell the folk:
When I am there
When I am not there
Have respect for my people

This woman leaves Barbados
That woman leaves Grenada
When I am there
When I am not there
Have respect for my people

With its references to Barbados and Grenada, the protest song above may also be classified as a migration song. Twenty-five of the 129 Big Drum songs also allude to foreign countries, and I group them similarly as migration songs. Ten of the twenty-five songs mention Ginade (Grenada) and its cities, L'Abbé (LaBaye or Grenville), Bacolet, and Gawé. The Grenadian hill Mt. Pandi is also specified. Seven songs refer to Trinidad and its oil-refining cities California, Guapo, and Arima. Three songs name Barbados and two mention the Venezuelan cities Barrancas and Lokain; Dominica and Aruba are referred to a single time each. References to the sites from which forced immigration of the earliest period occurred—Guinea, Dahomey, Kongo, and Haiti—occur within three songs from the era of slavery.

I have found a relationship between the numerical distribution of the country allusions in the songs and the prominence of the individual countries as migration magnets. Tabulating the named countries brings clarity to the argument over which island, Aruba or Trinidad, was the principal destination for migrating Carriacouans. As expected, there is multiple mention of Trinidad, but strangely, only one reference to Aruba, an island equally significant in its economic impact on Carriacou. Does this call my assumption about the accuracy of song as a historical tool into question? Not if we use the information correctly. It not only serves to attest to Aruba's role, but also corroborates the conjectured sequence of migrations. Rather than dismissing Aruba as an important territory for employment, it supports Hill's claim that Aruba was central only during a specific period, the late 1930s, and that Trinidad was more important over a longer period (Hill 1974:45). The Big Drum composition, moribund by the 1930s, could therefore not have reflected the shift in migration. In a subtle way, the absence of Aruba in the song texts strengthens my hypothesis that the 1920s saw the end of Big Drum composition.

Age of Songs

Though not conceived primarily as a diachronic, linear division of the repertoire, the song classification constructed by Pearse (see chapter 1) appears to codify the songs by age. I believe that Pearse attempted, rather, to separate, as the people themselves did, the Nation songs from the secular Creole repertoire. In isolating and categorizing the songs as Nation songs and Creole songs, he defined their individual functions and, in so doing, to some extent, their age. I suggest further that the first group, the Nation dances, reflect the homeland absorption, the longings, and the grief of the newly transplanted people. The post-emancipation Creole group reveals a consciousness of the need for bonding, social control, and pedagogy in the population. The third group, the Frivolous group, exhibits in its wealth of imported styles the depth of a longstanding social reality—the system of migration.

In the classification one finds the Kalenda, known as the earliest dance brought to the Americas, and the age-old Bongo on the list as Creole dances. Pearse rightly indicates their antiquity by calling them "old kalenda" and "old bongo."

The Frivolous group, like the Creole group, comprises compositions of the late nineteenth century but intersperses items composed up to the 1920s, the final age of Big Drum composition. This last group includes items appropriated by workers returning from sojourns in Grenada, Trinidad, Aruba, and Union Island and does not reflect the age of the songs. Updated variations of the ancient Kalenda and Bongo, the Trinidad Kalenda and Man Bongo, are included in this group. The importation of song, especially in the case of Trinidad borrowings, may have taken place over a protracted period, making the dating of imported Trinidad songs difficult.

The age of a song may be best detected from the subject matter and the personae in the texts. Beyond this, and only to a limited extent, the musical structure and setting of the poetic texts may help gauge the age of a song. The call and response, known to be the basic African choral form, exists in early as well as later songs in short or extended phrases.

The texts, with references to archaic deities, ancestors, and African empires, suggest their antiquity. The Bongo songs of separation ("Pléwé Mwe Lidé," "Maiwaz") and the Kongo song ("Kongo Beké") that invites the plantation proprietor to the dance clearly extend from the pre-emancipation era.

Other song types, surely as ancient as the Nation and Bongo types, carry texts that belie the age of the melodies. The lyrics were generated from modern incidents and composed within the Carriacou ideal, which praised, abused, and shamed members of the current society. To explain this superimposition of early-twentieth-century texts upon ancient melodies and offer an explanation for the endurance of old melodies, I engage the indigenous code of composition.

The doctor Loancine and the seine fisherman Sallo are remembered by the elderly, but the exact date of the song "Loancin-o" is derived from the date of the accident: 1901; and the date of the song "Sallo" is set by the tombstone inscription of Solomon Joseph (1914). In the same manner, Laza's death date establishes the composition date of the Hallecord "Laza" as 1888 (Pearse n.d.). The song "Madame Philip-o" dates prior to 1883, when the composer left for Grenada during the great three-year drought on Carriacou (Cudjo 1993).

A Kalenda, imported from Trinidad, is also easily dated (at least the words are), for it grew out of a Great Event. In the Trinidad riot of 1881, the people, led by the stickfighter Joe Talmana, fought the police and their notorious chief Captain Baker in a street battle over the right to hold carnival. Here is the original Kalenda, with its fast call-and-response pattern, followed by the Carriacou version.

Joe Talmana [Kalenda]

Cap'n Baker manday pou ou
Ah ya-yai, Joe Talmana
Cap'n Baker manday pou ou
Ah ya yai, Joe Talmana
Chorus: Ah ya yai, Tantie O-yo
Ah ya yai, Joe Talmana!
Ah ya yai, Joe Talmana (Elder 1966:106)

Captain Baker is asking for you
Ah ya-yai, Joe Talmana
Captain Baker is looking for you
Ah ya yai, Joe Talmana
Chorus: Ah ya yai, Aunt O-yo
Ah ya yai, Joe Talmana
Ah ya yai, Joe Talmana

Joe Talmana [Big Drum Kalenda]

Leader: [Fernando] mandé pu mwe
Chorus: Mwe wivé, Joe Talmana
Leader: Mwe wivé, Jab la, wivé
Chorus: Mwe wivé!

Leader: [Any name] is asking for me
Chorus: Here I am, Joe Talmana
Leader: Here I am, Devil, I'm here
Chorus: I'm here!

Less notorious characters, though memorialized in song, are lost to the society's memory. The people and incidents that have faded beyond the recall of the community, I suggest, were from a period long before the turn of the century.

Parang in Contemporary Composition

Although Big Drum composition has ended, the demand for songs aimed at reputation and social control persists. This domain and function has been usurped by another song genre, the Parang. It is a song type borrowed from Trinidad, which in turn had appropriated it from Venezuela. Parang performances occur every year during the Christmas season. The band parades through the streets, stopping to give unsolicited performances on the porches of homes, whose owners respond by offering rum and small gifts of money.

The male bands are made up of an assortment of string musicians playing guitars and *cuatros* (small, four-string guitars), biscuit box and bass drummers, and a bass horn player. The horn, the *baha* (a disposable 5 foot cardboard tube) imitates the bamboo pipe; and the bass drum, the *dup*, is a large cardboard barrel drum.

During the year Parang composers sort out the recent events and provide an open ear for gossip that might be used as themes for their new songs. During the Christmas season bizarre behavior, embarrassing interactions and ludicrous faux pas made by members of the community throughout the year are disclosed. The 1984 song "Pa Pig" recounts the theft of a pig and the sale of a butchered part of it by the thief—to the owner! A second parang, "Bounce Check," exposes the naivete of a woman who accepted a gift (a bad check) from an American marine in exchange for sexual favors. Some of the most comic songs are equally tragic and expose the negative side of human interaction and unfortunate, anti-social decision making.

These songs are often sung in public places (and now at Parang shows), and the audience, after a few hearings, learns them. Subjects of the ridicule must tolerate the disclosures; they have no recourse but to sing and dance the derisive tune along with the band and pretend to enjoy it. The power and honesty of the songs operates mainly through their comedic force, serving as a crucial social tool much as they must have served for nineteenth-century participants of the Big Drum. The threat of the exposure of betrayal, illicit sexual conduct, antisocial acts, or ignorance tightens social codes of behavior.

With a similar motive as the Parang, a Cheerup from the Big Drum,

"Lizibette Mauvais" ("Bad Lizibette"), scolds a mother for attending the dance instead of staying home with her children. A second Cheerup, "Mama, Don't Beat Me So, I Love Him Already," parodies the confusion of a mother at her daughter's sexual behavior. The punishment is too late, the young woman asserts, because she has already been to bed with her lover.

As early as 1947 Herskovits noted the thematic congruence in the Bélè, Bongo, Kalenda, and Calypso (Herskovits and Herskovits 1964:284). It is no surprise, then, that an early form of the Calypso, the Cariso, found its way from Trinidad to join the other topically oriented dance/songs within the Big Drum. In a similar way, Errol Hill points to the primacy of text composition in the Calypso, in which a limited number of tunes were repeated with textual variation (E. Hill 1972:72). And, strengthening the issue, historian Hollis "Chalkdust" Liverpoole (master calypsonian and winner of the title of Calypso Monarch) also mentions the practice in place during the 1930s and 1940s, where a corpus of tunes was shared and individually transformed by veteran calypsonians (Warner 1985:20).

I too posit direct musical relationships, but between the Big Drum song form and the Calypso, by examining the meaning and function of the traditional last line of the Calypso. The musical practice has been pondered for a long time, in which the verses of the early Calypsos ended with a shouted phrase: "*sans humanité!*" ("without mercy"). The Patois phrase is interpreted by Errol Hill as a translation of the Hausa word *kaiso*, meaning "you deserve no pity." The term gains in significance in the etymological search for the origin of the term *calypso*. Permutations of the Spanish word *caliso* (a topical, local song), the Patois term *wuso* ("to carouse"), and *kaiso* merged to form the term *calypso* (E. Hill 1967: 364). The Patois and Hausa words, essential to the discussion of the evolution of the Calypso, are often revived as an honorific shout, reminiscent of the ancient Patois practice and as an ovation for a great performance.

In drawing coherences between the ancient songs of the Big Drum and the Calypso, the term *sans humanité* may offer some substance for comparison. The word was sometimes heard as *sandimanité*, raising my suspicions about its relatedness to a term in the Big Drum, *salamani-o*. But more instructive than the relatedness of the word itself is how it was used. In the early Calypsos, *sans humanité* was the five-syllable last line, repeated at the end of each verse, that functioned as the organizing principle in the piece. With the decline in the use of Patois, *sans humanité* was supplanted by phrases such as "In this colony," "Every one and all," and "Britain rule the day" (E. Hill 1972:10), five syllables in each case. In the Cromanti Nation songs it is the single, final phrase in songs of petition sung on a single tone like a chanted response. We see the ubiquitous structure in the following songs and later in the Calypso "Grenada."

Ena-o [Cromanti]
Ena-o, Ena-o
Ena-o, mama nu
Salamani-o

Dondon, mwe Malade [Manding]
Ai, dondon
Mwe malade-o
Ai, dondon
Salamani-o

Ai, L'Abbe
Mwe malade-o
Ai, dondon
Salamani-o

Ai, voyé di l'Abbe
Mwe malade-o
Ai, dondon
Salamani-o

Oh, my friend
I am sick
Oh, my friend
Salamani-o

Oh, Grenville [Grenada]
I am sick
My friend,
Salamani-o

Oh, send and tell Grenville
I am sick
Oh, my friend
Salamani-o

The significance of the last line sways my interpretation of several last-line words in the Nation songs toward the more spiritual, African-language choice in translation, which includes "Dahomey," "Kongo," "Ambala," and "Sai Amba."

The Calypso as Ritual Successor

The most notable dimension inherited by the Calypso from ancient practice is the formal aspect of poetic structure. The short-phrased call and response, the stickfighting Kalenda type, recurs in modern war Calypsos as a revival of past practices. It is cleverly used by the premier calypsonian Mighty Sparrow to signify conflict in "Ten to One, is Murder" (Warner 1985:33). Called half-tone, this forceful structure was favored during the early years of Calypso composition. Other patterns, called whole-tone (a verse of four lines) and double-tone (the eight-lined stanza), are discussed by Quevedo (1983:20) for their poetic and stylistic ranges rather than for the formal evolutionary progression that I bring forward.

Recently challenged by the Reggae of Jamaica, the Calypso and its offshoot the Soca continue their reign as significant song forms of the Caribbean. The Calypso carries with it a rich traditional legacy of ritual song form, storytelling, grand eloquence, and political intent buoyed by the several cultural characteristics outlined by the cultural metaphor, Esu.

During the New Jewel movement, calypsonian Grantis "The Lion" Cudjo served as the movement's griot, traveling with Maurice Bishop on speaking tours to perform Calypsos that scorned American imperialism and intimidation. After the death of Bishop and the ultimate overthrow of the People's Revolutionary Government by the American invasion, his songs were no longer heard. However, the texts will inevitably come under the perusal of later historians who wish to capture the mood and motivation of that era.

With a historical purpose, the comic, insulting, and derisive songs sung by the People's Revolutionary Army long before the invasion of October 25, 1983, may be used to confirm the soldiers' anticipation of the event. During the pre-invasion period, I thought that their suspicion of President Reagan was a paranoid fantasy and that a military action of such magnitude would never be initiated. After the invasion my voice was stilled; however, the humor persisted in the army songs that alluded to the combat, but the focus shifted to self-derision. In the same vein, "See Soldier Run," a popular Parang of 1983, was sung not just by the Parang band but by Carriacouans at large who, with the song, parodied the flight of the outmatched PRA troops.

The Grenada Revolution of 1979 ended in 1983 with the murder of Prime Minister Maurice Bishop. During a rally to liberate him from house arrest he was assassinated by his own army along with five members of his cabinet and an unknown number of his adoring constituency. Curfews were quickly imposed, preventing the people from finding the incinerated bodies or witness their disposal. For many, therefore, the reality of the multiple deaths was never completely accepted.

After the death of Bishop, persons of various ranks reported mystical revelations. University-trained scholars as well as unlettered folk related the crowing of cocks at abnormal intervals as signals of treachery and interpreted their unusual visions as metaphysical phenomena.

Embellishments of the "Flying Africans" myth extend into contemporary thought to explain and integrate the unexplainable. Flight, as we have shown, was used as an explanation, not only for the disappearance of a runaway enslaved person, but for vanishing leaders as well. Julien Fedon disappeared after the revolution of 1795, leaving no trace. Though his military officers were captured and executed, Fedon mysteriously avoided custody and many conclude that he may have escaped by boat. Patrick Fermor, in his verbose interpretation of the people's thought, declares that he was "lifted into the sky as unvestigially as Enoch and Elijah" (Fermor 1950:192). Culture bearer Simeon Cudjo (1993) offers a parable in the voice of Fedon, a master of flight and "high science": "Souv kepay malewe qui pui chu mal mel qui pwe plan" ("Those who catch trouble must save themselves").

Much later, in the 1940s, the people anointed Marcus Garvey with the power of flight. Generating a rich body of myths (Chevannes 1991:123), Garvey's visionary bent, intensity, political acumen, and prophetic sensibility captured the imagination of the people. The myths, some planted by his own words, suggest his divinity and the righteousness of his cause. His philosophy, based upon a theology of liberation and repatriation, fostered the organization

15. "Revolution in Grenada—Fort Rupert—Dead by Gun Shot" by Canute Caliste.

of the Universal Negro Improvement Association. To this day his cause is fully embraced by the Rastafarian movement. After his imprisonment in America and before his self-exile in England, he sent a dramatic message to his supporters: "Look for me in the whirlwind or the storm, look for me all around you, for, with God's grace, I shall come and bring with me the countless millions of black slaves who have died in America and the West Indies and the millions in Africa to aid you in the fight for liberty, freedom, and life" (Clarke 1974:240). Because his body was never conclusively identified, it was thought that he remained alive and that his effectual avoidance of death and exile was actualized by flight.

The calypso "Grenada," written by the Mighty Sparrow, outlines the 1983 invasion of Grenada and the events leading up to the demise of Maurice Bishop and his Marxist party, the New Jewel Movement. This piece is a model of the functional history-keeping, news-broadcasting aspects found in many Caribbean song genres, including those of the Big Drum. I interpret the multi-verse calypso in the same way I explicated the texts of the more recondite single-strophe songs of the Big Drum, elucidating each verse in terms of my understanding of the Carriacouan perception of political action. It begins with the boast, it calls names, it accuses, it strikes metaphors, it employs double-voiced interpretations to tell the history and revise old forms—all of these are aspects of the practice of Signifyin(g).

Grenada

Verse 1: I want to go back to Grenada
To teach the Cubans how to fight
They let America take over
Complaining about Reagan's might
Lord, I hear everywhere
It's only bombs in the town
People running helter-skelter
Looking for a place to shelter
Señor, por favor

The voice of the song is sympathetic to Grenada, for the composer, though a resident of Trinidad, is an expatriate of Grenada. In his perspective, blame for the lack of resistance should be placed upon Cuba. Appropriately using Spanish where Patois was formerly used, he confronts Cuba throughout the song with the repeated last line choral formula of "Señor, por favor" or "Cuba, que pasa?" The five-syllable response functions much like the five syllables of *sans humanité* and sandimanité, reflecting a practice beloved by Grenadians and Trinidadians.

The chorus of "Grenada" introduces the personae in the personal and political drama. The antagonists in the play were Hudson Austin and Bernard Coard, who for years before and during the Marxist struggles were the closest allies of Prime Minister Bishop. Coard was born into a musical Carriacouan family that migrated to Grenada in the 1940s. He trained as a lawyer and grew to serve under his close friend as finance minister and deputy prime minister. His role in the national tragedy is that of the Judas (*Jida*), the traitor, for through him General Austin took the government by coup and also Bishop's life.

Carriacou's involvement in the political action was central. It nurtured not only ignoble presences like Coard's, but also positive personae. Herbert Blaize, the first prime minister of newly independent Grenada, was also a Carriacouan. He returned to the political arena through the electoral process in 1984 as prime minister to head the government shaken by the recent crisis.

The chorus of the calypso printed below portrays Coard as Judas, General Austin as Lucifer, and Phyllis, Coard's wife, as Jezebel. The main character, Bishop, as implied by the traitors surrounding him, is the Christ figure, who is deified upon his death.

The terminology "Judas" (Jida), "Lucifer" (Jab), and "traitor" resembles that in the Bélè Kawé songs of female conflict in which Jida and Jab betray the subject in a hypocritical way.

> Chorus:
> La manera que tengo mi corazon [From my perspective]
> Viva, viva la revolucion [Long live the revolution!]
> But if Cuba has arrested Coard and Austin
> America would not have excuse to come in
> Llevame a Grenada, Llevame [Take me back to Grenada, take me back]
> Judas, Lucifer and Jezebel mustn't get away

Philosophical differences heightened the struggle for leadership between Bishop and Coard, and their disagreements were public knowledge. Though also of the same basic orientation as Bishop, Coard was considered by Carriacouans a "hard-line" Marxist while Bishop was thought of as a humanitarian with the welfare of the masses at heart. Operating upon principles much further right on the socialist spectrum than his opposition would have him, Bishop seemed to be operating alone.

Factions in Bishop's government, critical of his method, conspired during his absence from Grenada, and upon his return placed him under house arrest. The charismatic leader was guilty, in the thinking of party members, of possessing "petit bourgeois tendencies," "one-manism," and a "cultism" that ignored the party dogma of fraternity. More radical elements of the party described him as a "sore-foot." They complained that from the commencement of the revolution he was awarded more "recognism" than the party body. "Amputation" of the sore foot was the only option.

The strength of the civil uprising of October 19 won the release of Bishop from house arrest, but the jubilant release mushroomed into the massacre in which Bishop, his cabinet members Jacqueline Creft, Unison Whiteman, Vincent Noel, Norris Bain, and Fitzroy Bain were slain. An unconfirmed number of civilians and children were also killed.

> Verse 2:
> Where them psychomaniacs come from
> To create so much bacchanal
> Who open the insane asylum
> And make a lunatic general
> Dusk to dawn, curfew on
> Wrong or right, shoot at sight
> Supported by construction workers
> With machine guns and rocket launchers
> Señor, por favor

The general referred to in the verse above is General Hudson Austin, organizer of the Revolutionary Military Council, which was established immediately after the assassination of Bishop. Directly after the slaughter, coup, and the takeover of Radio Grenada, the general announced a four-day curfew, and, as Sparrow truthfully reports, he threatened all people leaving their houses with being shot. It was presumed in Carriacou that the curfew was ordered to give cleanup crews the opportunity to discard the bodies of the slain citizens and the burned and unrecoverable body of Bishop.

The construction workers in verse 2 were the Cubans charged with supervising the building of Point Salines Airport. The workers fought beside Grenadian soldiers and were thought, at one time, to have been soldiers disguised as builders. The development of the airport was opposed by President Reagan, who felt that it threatened American security; it could be employed in military operations by Russian enemies. Its official intent, now slowly coming in sight, was the resurrection of Grenada's moribund tourist industry.

Verse 3 alludes to events prior to the New Jewel Revolution of 1979, when Prime Minister Eric Gairy and his private troops were in power. Gairy's administration was known for brutality, oppression, and financial scandals. Henchmen of Gairy called the "Mongoose Gang" led campaigns against other political factions, brutalizing individuals who opposed his policies.

The musical documentation of history in the song text lists peripheral players precisely. It names the leaders of the sister islands within the Organization of Eastern Caribbean States: John Compton (St. Lucia), Eugenia Charles (Dominica) and Edward Seaga (Jamaica). Tom Adams of Barbados, also an OECS member, was not on good terms with the Bishop government, nor did he respect Grenada's politics. On the other side, supporters and those tolerant of Grenada's politics (Guyana, Trinidad, and Belize) rejected the organization's plea for American intervention.

> Verse 3:
> Gairy squander all the money
> And the mongoose treat people like beast
> Then Bishop take over the country
> Through party traitors he's deceased
> Bajan [Barbadian] come,
> John Compton, Eugenia and Seaga
> Had to import Yankee soldiers to
> Stop the Grenada massacre
> Cuba, que pasa?

The political view offered in "Grenada" angered many Cubans, but it was held by the Mighty Sparrow alone, for the view of the majority of Grenadians and Carriacouans took an alternative slant. They placed no blame on Cuba, and the American forces were welcomed unequivocally. Horrified at the brutality exhibited by the Revolutionary Council and in fear of its next desperate act, the people embraced America as their savior.

Revolutionary ideals converge in slogans and songs. The slogan of the Fedon revolution, "Liberty, Equality, or Death," appropriated in the spirit of the French Revolution, remains a revolutionary ideal for many Grenadians (Sunshine 1982:19). In a parallel way, the motto of the New Jewel Revolution, "Forward Ever, Backward Never," has become a part of the historical past that indelibly marks the memory, especially of the young. In the same way that the Big Drum impacts memory by venerating ancestral heroes like Cromanti Cudjo, the calypso, parang, myth, Nancy stories, and the political slogan become compositional scores, praisesongs of cultural knowledge that enliven the ancestors and the disremembered.

Conclusion

With the primary goal of preserving and disseminating an example of early African ritual in the Americas, I have transcribed and translated the musical and poetic texts of the Big Drum of Carriacou, Grenada. Through musico/mythological analyses of the sensibilities in historical voices, another side, an internal, conceptual side of Caribbean history, is presented.

The Nation songs are testimony to the fact that during the desperate years of imprisonment the people of Carriacou danced not merely for the joy of movement but to petition their newly assembled pantheon of ancestors for deliverance. More than this, the repertoire reveals that their homeland longing for Guinea, Kongo, and Dahomey was intense and their suffering at familial severance deep. I suggest that the Big Drum helped to establish harmony in the new society and reassemble codes of inheritance, family, and lineage. The encoded songs reflect the pluralistic social organization of nine national groupings, which mirror the ethnic inheritances of the people.

Specific musical signals, essential and singular to the Big Drum, individualize the various nations. Strictly ordered rhythmic emblems codify the discrete division of ethnic inheritances and reflect the organizational structure of the society. Significantly, this system of musical memory enabled dispossessed people to reenter the community by joining a nation through avenues of musical inspiration. The affective response to a national rhythm may allow a marginal person to reclaim her nation, to reorganize an essential past shattered by the system of slavery. In this way, remarkably, the music and dance of this society served to bond, integrate, and reconstruct society and family. And, more remarkably, the ineffable concept of nation, preserved in the musical coding of rhythms, helped mediate systems of mental flight.

The Cromanti, with a commanding presence well documented in the literature of the West Indies, are perceived as socially dominant by their prominent place in the Carriacou ritual. As the first nation to call the ancestors in the Big Drum ritual, their position as leaders of the entire society is assumed. The essence of this primacy may be observed in the patterns of Akan name persistence (Quamina, Quashie, Cudjo) and from the structural implications of the Quashie genealogy presented here.

The work of Rattray on the Asanti, broadened and refined by scores of social scientists, holds great consequence in the analysis of Akan people in the "new world." The argument on the "Africanness" of the lineage system of Carriacou (see M. G. Smith) reopens the comparison between West African Asanti and Carriacou inheritance structures. The systems are not merely "similar" but a mirrored adaptation with many details and embellishments remaining intact. Thus, for the Carriacou system, the concept of dual inheritance remains an impervious "grid," with the father rather than the mother donating the "blood" to the offspring. Though the structure was transformed when the patrilineal code overtook the matrilineal in the Cromanti lineage system, the African base in the dual-soul logic was not altered, nor were its meaning and ancillary configurations weakened.

Aside from the sociological investigation of the Cromanti, I attempt to compare the ethnic stereotypes in Caribbean literature with the inner statements of the parabolic song texts. However, the Igbo data pose a problem. The defiant and recurrent song phrase in Igbo songs ("nothing can harm the Igbo") and the colonial descriptions of the Igbo are at odds. More than any of other nations, the Igbo were widely described as diffident, despondent, and suicidal. Their behavior may have been misrepresented in historical documents, and the "fixed melancholy" perceived in them may have reflected a final, audacious, political stance of resistance rather than the despondency of dependency.

In tracing the non-Patois terms in the Nation songs to Hausa, Arabic, or Yoruba, I see in them evidence of far-flung cultural appropriations as the result of invasions within African contexts and widespread language infiltration through trade and ritual exchanges. The unsettled questions about ritual integration and accommodation seem especially pertinent to the preservation of the terms: Sari Baba, Ena, Oko, Negesse Manding, Amba, Igbo Lele, Webe Nu, Salamani, Sai Amba, Ahwusa Wele, Anancy, Pa Beni, Kanjuri, Kanbera, and Abadino. The word origins presented are conjectural, but they point, somehow, to multiple influences, ethnic accommodation, and a thoughtful, conscious assemblage, by and large, of ancestral options.

The symbols of the dance also reflect mental involvement with the past. First, the cyclephonic texture of the music, in itself, revives not only history, but, in its ritual role, invites beings from the spirit world into the world of the living. The immutability of the music is explained by its function—to entertain a spirit audience appreciative and responsive to signals from the past: bell-gong motives, cyclic polyphony, and responsorial vocal interplay.

Further, the latent symbolism surrounding the *saraca* meals, the absence of salt from ritual food and the act of sprinkling ritual rum converge with the musical symbols to reify and promote spirit flight. The dance, too, reveals the soaring image of the bird in the cool face and intrepid movements of winged-skirted dancers. Culture bearers themselves express the aesthetics of Creole dance: "dance with melody, grace, sweetness, like something good to eat, like a brave turkey-cock—or like a cool, sleeping top."

The search for word etymologies is central to my study for it may uncover conceptual ideologies and a social logic as well. In the review of the greater rituals, Orisa, Vodun, Santeria, and Winti, we find that they are named after the culturally accepted concept for spirit. Ancestral rites, however, are named after the drum: the kele, kutumba, grand tambour, tambu, big drum, gwo ka. Among these the exceptions are few—the reel, Jombee, and the Sango rituals are named, respectively, after an Anglo dance, the spirits, and the awesome Yoruba spirit of thunder and lightening.

Yoruba danced religions universally share not only an ideology in naming practice but also the incomparable convention of spirit manifestation. The form of the practice, common in the Yoruba religions, is distinct from that found among others such as the Spiritual Baptists. The equally significant "dream request" celebrated by most religious communities and even in the "invented tradition" of Rastafarianism, also mirrors a most revered and ancient tradition. But, opposing the uniformity of other religions, Rastafarians proclaim the liberation message overtly—a message of repatriation that remains concealed in all other ritualized mediums.

I employ Henry Louis Gates's unifying literary theory, which centers upon the ritual figure Esu Elegba (a Yoruba/Dahomean cultural emblem), to explain ritualization in African-American language, communication, music, and dance. The linguistic play of Signifyin(g) may be used not only in the interpretation of African-American culture but also to understand the African diaspora and, most successfully, in specific genres like the calypso and ritual songs. Even more important, the Gates theory may be used as a metaphor for and explanation of the self-reliant acts of social amalgamation and artistic, lingual, and ritual creolization that occur in the creation of new models.

The debate over the "Africanness" of the Carriacou lineage is most strongly argued by the survival of concepts held by the people themselves. Even without engaging clear-cut West African lineage prototypes or rigorous historical census documents, the ancillary ritual symbols created by crossed dance towels, rum libations, salt metaphors, the *saraca* offering, etymologies, African names, lineage "reversals," the bell-gong and drum, and other obvious, Signifyin(g) African conceptual and musical continuities, we see African meaning and intent in the Big Drum. But beyond these symbols, "what people say [or sing] of their origins, think about their connectedness and embrace as their tradition remain the most telling information sources" (Robertson 1984).

From the broad thematic issues and implications in the people's song texts, I conjecture that the Big Drum represented and exerted a high level of influence as a religious tool, social organizer, political space, and personal cathartic agent. The people sang to mediate the confusion found in their new powerless position, drummed to find solutions to the multiple layers of social conflict, and danced to define a personal system of flight. The myth of the Flying Africans hovers over political memory as well as the spiritual world of flight in the Caribbean. The dance ring was the spiritual space within which the people mediated the tolerance of differences, worked through the several modes of rebellion, and created personae that could survive within the strictures, threats, and dehumanizing conditions of the slave experience.

Thus, the dance event, the parang songs, and the calypsos of eras past, with their shared tone of *mespris*, *picong*, and *fatigue*, helped restore the fragmented personality. Song helped to remodel bonds of friendship, family structures, and the broadest intrastructure of post-emancipation society itself.

The concept of nation as elucidated by the song collection refers to dimensions outside mere geographical affiliation. The concept is an affirmation, despite language loss and regional displacement, of social, spiritual and ancestral systems. Several varied national ideals may be interpreted from the organization of West Indian dances, whose frameworks, whether loosely or carefully designed, may call forth a general interpretation of the society's structure. In the Carriacou case the discrete though integral nature of the dance ring suggests a democratic social ideal that honors national exclusivity, yet celebrating social plurality. I propose that the Big Drum was the consolidating forum of an international congress of people who, "Even when the spirit took hold and their souls and writhing bodies seemed about to soar off into the night, their feet remained planted firm" (Marshall 1983:34).

Appendix 1
Big Drum Song List

Appendix 1 contains a list of the 129 songs and song fragments that serve as the basis of this study. Song titles are listed in the left column; the numbers in parentheses after some of the titles are from the index of songs compiled by Donald Hill (1973:879). The songs are grouped by nation or dance type with titles taken from the personal name in the song text or the first phrase of the song.

The abbreviations in the middle column indicate whether the songs appear on recording by Fernandez (F), Hill (H), Lomax (L), or Pearse (P). These recordings are listed in the bibliography. The last column is a list of themes pertaining to each song, abbreviated as follows:

AV   Ancestor Veneration
BP   Beg Pardon
C   Consolation
GE   Great Event
LA   Lament
M   Migration
PI   Picong or Derision
PR   Protest
S   Satire
SC   Social Control
W   Wanga or Distrust

Some texts receive two classifications, and those that are indeterminate and parabolic are not classified by theme.

Songs	Recordings	Themes
Arada		
Derika (H-22)	P	
Do Ré Mi Dé	F	
Banda		
Me No Yeri-o	L	
Quashie No Dey-o (Bayan-o)		
Bélè Kawé		
Ai, Ai, Salli Hundé	L	W
Ami-al-o		
Dandi-é Yé, Alé Mandé Jida (H-28)	P	W
Dandi-é Yé (Tan Clarris-o)	F	W
Depi ta Gawé alé-o		GE
Lawen Dama-o		
Nora	L	SC
Lawen Matulé (H-29)	P	W
Moka Dodo		M
Bongo		
De Lenmi ba ka di Bonju		W
Engine Train Delis-o	F	M
La Ginade-o		M
Mené Mwe Cont(e) (H-6)		BP
Oyo, Mama, Bel Louise-o (H-46)	P	LA, M
Pléwé Mwe Lidé (H-45)	L, P	C, M
Maiwaz	L	C
Man Bongo		
In My Own Native Land (H-48)	P	PR
Boula (Quelbe)		
William-o		
Cariso		
Mwe Ba t'ni Mama Ici		M, PR
Chamba		
Ai-o, Kanjurio	P	AV
Ananci-o Kumarie'	P	AV
Chamba Dumfries (H-24)		
Cheerup		
Call Saireel, Girl		SC
Lizibette Mauvais		S
Mama, Don't Beat Me So,		
I Love Him Already		SC
Mary and Martha (H-50)	L	SC

Songs	Recordings	Themes
Petit Solomon		S
Titiri-o, Surrender		SC
You Tell a Lie		SC
Chiffoné		
Femme Ka Chiffoné (H-49)	P	S
Cromanti		
Anancy-o, Sari Baba (H-5)	F, L	AV, BP
Anancy Cudjo	L	
Cromanti Cudjo (H-4)	H	AV, BP
Midnight Cromanti		
Abadino	L	BP
Ena-o (H-3)	F, P	BP
Oko (H-2)	L	BP
Ahwusa Webé Nu		AV, BP
Pa Beni	P	AV, BP
Gwa Bélè		
Captain Desbat (H-30)	P	GE
La U C'est (H-55)		W
Madame Philip-o (H-33)	F	W
McIntyre (Captain Desbat)		LA
Mwe Di No		W
Mwe Malade Ayo	L	
Sandy Island		GE
Hallecord		
Drummer Mwe		LA
Envetta-o		M
Fantasi-o		SC
Helé, Mwe Plewé (H-37)	P	LA
Laja, Ai Laja-o (H-36)	P	MW
Lawen Victoria		PI, S
Laza	L	
Levé Ju 'vé Ju		
Loancin-o		LA, M
Mama Bedeau Ka Helé		LA, W
Na Goli-o		LA
Police Lawen		LA
Rainbow		LA
Sesé Ani-o Levé-o	L	LA
Sylvi Ka Mandé (H-35)	P	M
Vagabond Jane		

Songs	Recordings	Themes
Igbo		
E-o Igbo, Lé-lé (Grenadian Song)		AV
Hausa Welé	L	AV
Iama Diama Igbo Lé-lé (H-8)	L	AV
Igbo Ginade-o (H-12, 13)	L	M
Igbo Mauvais Nation (Grenadian Song)		PI
Igbo Volé (Petite Martiniquan Song)		S
Igbo Wan Dem (H-9)	H	SC
Ovid-o, Bagadé (H-10)	F, L	C, W
Ton Ton Banan Moka Pilé		
Juba		
Ju Noel Nu Kai Dancé Gawe (Kawé) (H-54)	H,L	M
Le Ouè Mwe La		M, PR
Oyo, Voyé Di Lawen Baby (H-51)	P	GE
Kalenda		
Amwé Beké	L	M
Barrancas-i-o		M
Captain Simon		PI
Digel		M
Joe Talmana (H-43)	L	PR
In The Morning When I Wake		S
Norman Amba Glo		SC
Tim Bwai-o-ai-o (H-41)	P	W
Today, Today		LA, M
Youn Bois		M
Man Kalenda		
Amba Pier Coco		SC
Corporal William		SC
Panama		M
Woman Kalenda		
Antoin-o		
Beausejour-ai-o		W
Helé-i-o		W
Voyé Di-o Bucalé		W
Kongo		
[Crom]anti Couro (H-16)	P, L	AV
Kongo Beké (H-15)		SC
Kongo Malabu		AV
Kongo Tululu (H-14)		SC

Songs	Recordings	Themes
Manding		
Maria-o Bakolet	L	M
Mary Rengdeng-o		M
Negesse Manding, Saiamba		AV
Dondon Mwe Malad-o, Salamani (H-21)		LA, M
Viola		
Moko		
C'est Mwe Nani Moko (H-19)	L	
U Mwe Ba Filé (H-20)	P	
Piké		
Ai, Simon Dico		
Eleno		SC
Jeune Fille Ki Passé La		S
Oh, Mary, Who You Breeding For?		PI
Popo Ave Orelia		PI
Tan tan Reigner		PI
Tewé Wanga La U Meté		W
Viola (H-57)		
Temné		
Temné Woman-o (H-17)	L	SC
Zabette Lundi (H-18)	P	SC
Unclassified songs and fragments		
Ai, Liza		
All Over (Powder Dance) (H-59)		
Angie Desbat		S
Anna Number One		M
Babado		M
I Want Me Courtin' Chair		S
Irene Make the Baby When the Corporal Came		PI
Jean Pickin' Cotton An Ting		
Laureston, Levé		M
Mama Mary With Obeah Bag		M, S
Mesir Welsh		S
Petit Solomon		S
Sallo (H-58)		SC, W
Secret Song; When I Go		

Appendix 2
Glossary

Amwe Beké. Urgent plea for help.

Ancestor. African conceptualization of the family's deceased, a spirit presence influential in the lives of its descendants.

Ajoupa. Carib term in Carriacou speech meaning "hut" or "edifice."

Arada. Ethnic group; Dahomean city (Allada, Ardrah).

Baban Salla (Babbar Salla). The Hausa ceremony also known as "The Greater Feast."

Baboula. Early name for the drum in the French Antilles; a Caribbean dance.

Baja. Mouth-blown bass instrument made of bamboo or commercial cardboard tubing. The player's lips are the vibrating element.

Bamboula. Dance event of the nineteenth-century Antilles.

Banda. Ethnic group; Haitian dance; Big Drum dance/song classification.

Beg Pardon. Text classification; ritual of propitiation.

Beké, Bakra, Bukra. White person; mixed-race person; a wealthy person; a person with European taste or style

Bélè. Creole dance.

Big Drum (Nation Dance). Dance/song ritual of Carriacou.

Big Time. Large feast; ritual.

Bobol. Illegal trade, inter-island smuggling.

Boli. Gourd used in making the *chac-chac.*

Bongo. Creole dance.

Boula. The two drums in the Big Drum set that control the nation beat.

Brave. Smart, industrious.

Break. Rhythmic change in the cutter's improvisation.

Bunjé. God; derived from the French *Bon Dieux*

Bush medicine. Traditional healing practice incorporating herbs.

Callaloo. Traditional West Indian food; a green vegetable; soup/sauce

Calypso. Caribbean vocal form originating in Trinidad.

Cane row. Woven hairstyle called corn rows in North America.

Cantique. French hymnody sung at prayer meetings.

Canzo. Second level of the several initiations of Haitian vodun.

Chac-chac. Boli maraca played by the chantwell.

Chamba. Ethnic group; Big Drum dance and song classification

Chantwell. Singer/dancer; leader of the Big Drum.

Chattam. Frivolous dance of the Big Drum.

Cheerup (Chirrup). Frivolous dance of the Big Drum.

Chiffoné. Frivolous dance of the Big Drum.

Compose. To lead and extemporize a Big Drum song.

Coupé Cou ("Cut Throat"). A minor ritual within the Big Drum that is now lost.

Coolie. Vernacular name for East Indian person—no longer acceptable.

Coucou. Traditional food staple of ground corn

Creole. Person born in the West Indies; a Big Drum dance grouping; a language or cultural idiom generated from two distinct ethnic sources.

Cromanti. Ethnic group; Gold Coast factory for enslaved people; Big Drum dance/song classification

Cuatro. Four-stringed instrument that is plucked and strummed.

Cut. To beat, play, hit or strike; to "roll" or produce florid statements on the drum.

Cutter (cot, cut, cutter, kupé, coupé). Center drum of the Big Drum ensemble; animal surgeon; eighteenth-century sloop

Czien (zien, zanguien). Spider; an Akan-derived Anancy story.

Deliso! Exclamation of delight used by the singer.

Dodo la! Exclamation to the dancer: "Sleep like a top!"

Douette. Nineteenth-century French costume retained by female Big Drum dancers.

Dream. Message, appearance, or communication by the spirit of a deceased family member.

Dup. Large cardboard barrel drum.

Ent. In English Creole: "not, ain't."

Fatigue. To tease; to "give" fatigue.

Fete. Ceremony, feast.

Firelight! Singers' exclamation within a song.

Free ring. The introductory time segment reserved for the ancestors' dance.

Fulé. Boula drum

Ganga. Old head female guard of the parents' plate.

Giné. African person.

Gini (Guinea). Africa.

Grand tambour. The early Antillean drum; the big drum

Guide. Saphie or amulet worn as protection.

Gwa Bélè (Grand Belair). Creole dance.

Gwa moun. Old people; the ancestral generation.

Hallecord. Creole dance of the Big Drum.

Humbug. To annoy or bother a person.

Ianman Igbo Lélé. Haitian Igbo deity.

Igbo Lélé. Haitian Igbo deity.

Jab. Patois term for "devil."

Jablesse. Single-hoofed female witch who pursues children and taunts men.

Jack Iron. Overproof rum used in Big Drum libations.

Jammette. Boisterous woman; low-class woman.

Jida. "Judas"; betrayer.

Jig Igbo. Syncretized dance in the Big Drum.

Juba. Big Drum Creole dance; black dance of the Caribbean and southern United States.

Juju. Witchcraft employing doll fetishes.

Ka (Quart). Patois word for "drum."

Kaiso. Hausa word, possibly related to the origins of the word *Calypso*, meaning "one more time."

Kalenda, Calinda. Creole dance of the Big Drum; ancient Kongo dance types.

Kata (cutter). the center drum of the Big Drum drum trio; head pad used under loads carried on the head (Twi); the Kongo instrumental style using the body of an instrument as a drum.

Kawé. Dance position or style, from the French *carre*; defense position in the stickfight.

Kokoma. Sickness derived from witchcraft.

Kongo. Ethnic group; an African person; Big Drum dance/classification.

Langage. Ritual language, glossolalia.

Lawen. Queen; female honorary head of the dance event.

Lawen Juba. Queen of the dance.

Lé-lé. To turn in the dance; to beat with sizzle stick.

Lendi Béké. First working day; Monday.

Lenmi (Lelmi). The enemy.

Long Time People. Former generations now deceased.

Lora. Frivolous dance in the Big Drum.

Lougarou (Loupgarou, Legarou). Flying male witch.

Mabouya. Carib word meaning "evil spirit"; lizard; island near Carriacou.

Maljo. "Evil eye"; a hex projected by a glance; derived from the French *mal yeux*.

Mama Nu. Female deity, "our mother."

Man Bongo. Frivolous dance in the Big Drum.

Manding. Ethnic group; Mandingo; dance/song classification

Mash. Foot movement in the dance.

Mbakara. Ibibio and Efik word meaning "white man"; one who surrounds or governs.

Mespris. To tease.

Moko. Ethnic group; Big Drum dance/song classification.

Maroon. Communal work project; sacrifice to pray or give thanks for rain; Beg Pardon propitiatory ritual.

Move with. To associate with.

Move well. To get along well with another person.

Nancy (Anancy). Traditional stories of the West African type.

Nation dance. The Big Drum.

Nation dances. Oldest group of Big Drum dances comprising the nine national dance types.

Nation songs. Song group comprising the nine national African types.

Nation. Ethnic division; cultural tradition.

Neg. Black person.

Ntoro. In the Akan conception, the spiritual inheritance donated by the father.

Obeah. Witchcraft involving paraphernalia.

Old head. Older person versed in culture knowledge.

Old hoe. Bell or gong in the Big Drum ensemble, which may be a hoe blade or any piece of metal.

Old parents. Ancestors who are thought to take part in human activities.

Pan. Tin drum used in the parang ensembles; Trinidad steel drum ensemble.

Parents' Plate. Ritual food offering for ancestors.

Picong. To tease and deride; a text classification.

Piké. Frivolous dance in the Big Drum.

Paisadé. Woven pattern in the African house; quadrille dance step.

Powers. African gods.

Prayer meetings. Funeral rites or wakes held on the 3rd, 9th, and 40th nights after death.

Provisions. Basic foodstuffs; agricultural staples.

"Put it." To begin a song is to "put it."

Quadrille, English quadrille. Square-formation dance accompanied by European fiddle melodies; dance popular in nineteenth-century Europe accompanied by musical figures.

Reggae. Contemporary West Indian song style originating in Jamaica.

Reigner. "Loose" woman of questionable standards.

Ring. Dance area; the circle formed by onlookers.

Roll. To make special cadences on the drum.

Roll rice. Molded rice used in the Parents' Plate offering.

Sacrifice. Animal slaughter for ritual feeding; food offering of the Parents' Plate; ritual of thanksgiving or Beg Pardon.

Salamani. Possibly related to an Arabic greeting; Hausa word meaning "the middle of the night."

Saraca, Salaca, Sacara. Ritual feeding of the ancestors; a feast that acknowledges the tradition of "feeding the children."

Scotch Igbo. Syncretized Big Drum dance.

Sea egg. Sea urchin found among rocks in the sea, eaten as a delicacy.

Second Burial. In Igboland, the symbolic spirit burial of the deceased that occurs years after death in Igboland, Nigeria.

Shango hair cutting. Yoruba-based ritual borrowed from Grenada that involves the cutting of a specific hair type thought to be an evil omen for the child.

Slack. "Loose," careless person.

Smoke food. Food cooked outdoors over a three-stone fire.

Sukayan. Flying witch that searches for human blood.

Spirit. Deceased person.

Stone Feast. The final death observance that includes the laying of the tombstone.

Temné. Ethnic group; dance/song classification.

Three-stone cooking. Ritual cooking on outdoor fireplace where pots are placed between three large stones.

Title. Last name.

Trinidad Kalenda. Dance type; Frivolous dance.

Wake. First funeral observance in a series of five observances.

Wanga. Malevolent hex.

Webe no (nu). Phrase used to call the spirits.

Wet the ground. To throw rum libations on the earth.

Wheel. To rotate in the dance.

Winding. Hip gyrations in dance.

Wiss. Strong vines used in securing drum head.

Wulé. To revolve in dance; to roll; to broadcast news.

Yard. Communal, ritual, and social space surrounding the house.

Zien (Czien). Akan spider; the Anancy story.

Notes

1. Runagate Nation

1. The origin of the use of the fiddle as a dance instrument is explored by Sterling Stuckey in *Slave Culture*. Employing the trickster tales, he shows that the violin was not simply a functional carryover of the drum but possibly a survival of ancient musical practices.

2. The meaning of the term *creole* varies. First used to designate a white person born in the Caribbean, it evolved to pertain to any people other than immigrant Africans. In Louisiana and in the nineteenth-century Caribbean it referred to the separate, mixed-race group. Today it is less a racial term for it is usually associated with newly formed languages and cultural practices generated out of European and African contact. In the Big Drum, the nineteenth-century dances and songs with syncretic ideals of music and movement are classified as Creole.

2. Sleepers Awake!

1. Of the many researchers who explored the dual exogamic system of the Asanti, C. S. Rattray stands in the forefront with his seminal research on the Asanti nation. Besides Rattray, Melville Herskovits, Meyer Fortes, Eva Meyerwitz, J. B. Danquah, M. Field, K. A. Busia, Margaret Mead, Charles Wooding, Donald Hill, Ken Bilby and a host of others aimed their discussions on the clarification, reversal of analyses, or the employment of the major formulations in the social analysis of cultures of the American Akan Diaspora. Within the Asanti social code of dual inheritance Rattray analyzes the personal endowment of the *ntoro, abusua, mogya,* and *sunsum,* and *kra.* He defines the *ntoro* as the "male totemic spirit which every child, male or female, inherits from its father" and the *abusua* as the clan or *mogya* ("blood"). The fusing of the two, then, represents a metaphor of the physiological aspect of conception.

2. In her introductory essay "African Mythology," Alice Werner created an extraordinary survey of the origins and permutations in the meaning of the word *kata*. The underlined phrase toward the end of her essay has special meaning in this chapter's

discussion of material and conceptual structures. The cultural artifacts of music, dance, and ritual may be experienced as particular to a culture, but, as Werner suggests, the most intimate knowledge of a culture is often not expressed by the people at all for the historical notions that created the symbols may continue half-forgotten and fragmented.

> Let us take the case of the Zulu word *inkata* and the thing denoted by it. The word is also found in Nyanja as *nkata*, in Swahili *khata* . . . in Chwana as *khare* . . . in Herero as *ongata*, and in similar or cognate forms elsewhere. Its original meaning seems to be a "coil" or "twist." But it generally stands for the twisted pad of grass or leaves used by people who carry heavy loads on the head. But the Zulu *inkata* has another and more recondite meaning. The *inkata yezwe* ("coil of the country") or *inkata yomuzi* ("coil of the clan") is both a symbol of unity and federation of the people and an actual talisman to ensure the same, together with the personal safety of the chief. It is a large twist or cushion of grass, impregnated with powerful "medicines" and made with special ceremonies by professional "doctors." At other times it is kept, carefully hidden from view, in the hut of the chief wife. I do not know whether the *inkata* has everywhere the same ritual significance. I strongly suspect that, where such is not recorded, it has either become obsolete or escaped the notice of inquirers, as—*belonging to the most intimate and sacred customs of the people—it would be quite likely to do.* But, in Uganda, *enkata* means, not only the porter's head-pad, but the top-most of the grass rings forming the framework of the house and supporting the thatch. . . . Now, we find that, on the Gold Coast, where the head-pad is called *ekar* in Twi, it has some ritual connection with the succession to the chieftainship. (emphasis mine)

3. Lavé Tete

1. The definition of the Haitian *Lave Tete* ritual varies. In *The Drum and the Hoe*, Courlander explains that all people are born with a personal *loa* ("spirit"): "Should a man acquire a new loa to replace the old . . . he must undergo a ceremony known as *Lave tete*—the 'washing of the head'." Katherine Dunham, in contrast, takes another perspective in *Dances of Haiti* by reviewing the initiation rites in a personalized way: "My previous two baptisms were of *lave tete* (head-washing to remove my former unclean, or uninitiated self from my head, leaving it free to retain properties inducted during the ceremony or to receive the *loa*, or gods, without physical danger to myself)." Dunham also comments on the translation of the first invocation used as the first epigraph to chapter 3: "'Papa Legba, open barrier for me, life sends good things for me'. Or it could be that life demands good things, depending on how the creole is translated" (Dunham 1969:120). The second epigraph, taken from *Also Sprach Zarathustra*, was quoted by Dunham in chapter 7 of *Island Possessed*.

2. The *bembe* instrumentation includes a drum, *guiro* (*agbes*), and iron bell. The more formal *guemilere* ceremony uses the hourglass *bata* drums and *achere* rattle.

3. Zora Neale Hurston alone documents the double drum name, *kata katumba*, in "Baracoon," an unpublished biography of Cudjo Lewis (Moorland-Spingarn Research Center, Howard University Library, 1931).

4. See Kolinsky's analysis of Suriname music (Herskovits and Herskovitz 1936:520) for an interpretation of the power of the drum to call the gods, to articulate divine messages, and to send them back.

5. The metaphor of the rider, charged with sexual imagery, surrounds the act of possession. The equestrian analogy, too, undergirds the vision of the deity "mounting" the devotee, the horse. Margaret Thompson Drewel recounts the action during the possession of an Ogun medium of Igbogila, Nigeria, whose associates bind and "saddle" the medium, pulling, tightening and securing cloths to secure him before the journey (Drewel 1992:183). This scene calls to mind the Trinidad Orisa manifestation described above, where the attendants rush to prepare the "horse" before being ridden. They remove her glasses and jewelry, tightly binding her stomach with her shawl, ostensibly to avoid physical harm to herself.

Although I wish to limit the comparison between Caribbean danced religions and practices in North American churches, the two processes of "saddling" may be seen as coherent. In many North American churches, white-suited and -capped "nurses" surround the person imbued with the Holy Ghost and relieve her of potentially harmful personal objects, allowing movement but protecting her from self-injury simply by forming a ring around her. The following description of the sanctified dance of urban African-American churches is from James Baldwin's *Go Tell It on the Mountain*:

> The power struck someone, a man or woman; they cried out, a long wordless crying, and, arms outstretched like wings, they began the Shout. Someone moved a chair a little to give them room, the rhythm paused, the singing stoppped, only the pounding feet and clapping hands were heard; then another cry, another dancer; then the tambourines began again, and the cries rose again, and the music swept on again, like fire, or flood, or judgment. Then . . . like a planet rocking in space, the temple rocked with the Power of God.

6. The Juba was a dance complex and a rhythm known widely throughout the black diaspora. Sterling Stuckey states in *Going Through the Storm*, p. 71:

> Thomas Talley describes "two dancers in a circle of men" with the following lines being patted:
>
> > Juba circle, raise de latch
> > Juba dance that Long Dog Scratch
> > Juba! Juba!

> Though that description was based on its performance in the south, it was an African dance formation—one possibly named after Juba, the city in Sudan—and rhythmic pattern, though drums were not used to get percussive effects. According to Frederick Douglass, slaves in Maryland explored the theme of injustice to Juba rhythms.

One of the few protest songs of the Big Drum, "Le Oue Mwe La" (see chap. 4) is also a Juba, danced by two women.

7. Marshall employs the same clash of waters by manipulating the currents at Kick 'em Jenny as a metaphor of internal conflict in her novel. See Pollard (1985:285–98).

4. Beg Pardon

1. Helen Roberts points to the convention of elongated word endings in the Jamaican Kromanti repertory (1926). The comparison of the overlooked practice in song traditions could be a fertile area for black diasporan musical research.

2. Babies afflicted with *maljo* grow limp and may eventually die. People report that Loancine as well as other practitioners would first prick the child with a needle to test its responsiveness. Then, with her vast selection of herbal combinations, she would bring babies back to life, often bathing the children, according to custom, in cochinille (*Nopapea cochenellifera*) extract. The prescription for prevention of *maljo* was washing blue, camphor, and garlic sewn within a small bag to be hung around the child's neck. The bagged prophylactic against evil, the *guide*, sometimes contained *acefecita* (*acefesida*), a plant substance (*Ferula assafoetida*) that is also used in the southern part of the United States in similar ways as outlined above as a protection against colds.

Bibliography

Amira, John, and Steven Cornelius. 1992. *The Music of Santeria: Traditional Rhythms of the Bata Drums*. Crown Point, Ind.: White Cliffs Media Co.

Abraham, Roy Clive. *Dictionary of the Hausa Language*. 1962. London: University of London Press.

Abrahams, Roger D., and John Szwed, eds. 1983. *After Africa: Extracts from British Accounts and Journals of the Seventeenth and Nineteenth Centuries Concerning the Slaves, Their Manners and Customs in the British West Indies*. New Haven and London: Yale University Press.

Adams, C. Ferguson "Sugar." 1983. Personal communication.

Andrews, Estimie. 1983–93. Personal communications.

Andrews, Gentle. 1983. Personal communication.

Barrett, Leonard. 1976. *The Sun and the Drum: African Roots in Jamaican Folk Tradition*. London: Heineman.

Bell, Hesketh J. 1893. *Obeah, Witchcraft, in the West Indies*. London: Sampson, Low, Marston.

Benjamin, Roy. 1983. Personal communication.

Bilby, Kenneth, and Fu-Kiau Kia Bunseki. 1983. "Kumina: A Kongo-Based Tradition in the New World." *Les Cahiers du Cedaf*. Brussels: ASDOC-Studies 8, vol. 4.

Bowdich, T. Edward. 1819. *Mission from Cape Coast to Ashantee*. London: J. Murray.

Brinkley, Frances. 1978. "An Analysis of the 1750 Carriacou Census." *Caribbean Quarterly* 24, nos. 1–2 (March–June): 44–60.

———. 1987. Personal communication.

———. n.d. Brinkley Papers. Carriacou, Grenada. In the author's possession.

Busia, Abena P. A. 1989. "What Is Your Nation?: Reconnecting Africa and Her Diaspora through Paule Marshall's *Praisesong for the Widow*." In *Essays on Criticism, Theory, and Writing by Black Women*, edited by Cheryl Wall. New Brunswick, N. J.: Rutgers University Press.

Carr, Andrew. 1953. "A Rada Community in Trinidad." *Caribbean Quarterly* 3, no. 1.

Cassidy, Frederic G. 1961. *Jamaica Talk: Three Hundred Years of the English Language in Jamaica*. London and New York: Macmillan & Co. and St. Martins Press.

Cérol, Marie-Josée. 1992. "What History Tells Us about the Development of Creole in Guadeloupe." *New West Indian Guide/Nieuwe West-Indische Gids* 66, nos. 1–2: 61–76.

Cevannes, Barry. 1991. "Garvey Myths among the Jamaican People." In *Garvey: His*

Work and Impact, edited by Rupert Lewis and Patrick Bryan. Trenton, N.J.: Africa World Press.

Charles, Oliver. 1991. Personal communication.

Clarke, John Henrik. 1974. *Marcus Garvey and the Vision of Africa*. New York: Vintage.

Clifford, James. 1997. *Routes: Travel and Translation*. Cambridge and London: Harvard University Press.

Corion, Jones "Pofella." 1983–86. Personal communications.

Courlander, Harold. 1960. *The Drum and the Hoe*. Berkeley and Los Angeles: University of California Press.

Cox, Edward. 1984. *Free Coloreds in the Slave Societies of St. Kitts and Grenada, 1763–1833*. Knoxville: University of Tennessee Press.

Crow, Hugh. 1830. *Memoirs of the Late Captain Hugh Crow of Liverpool; Comprising a Narrative with Descriptive Sketches of the Western Coast of Africa; Particularly Bonny; the Manners and Customs of the Inhabitants, the Productions of the Soil, and the Trade of the Country, to Which are Added, Anecdotes and Observations, Illustrative of the Negro Character*. London: Longman, Rees, Orme, Brown and Green; and G. and J. Robinson.

Cudjo, Simeon. 1993. Personal communication.

Curtin, Phillip D. 1969. *The Atlantic Slave Trade: A Census*. Madison and London: University of Wisconsin Press.

Da Costa, Adrian. 1984. Personal communication.

David, Christine. 1979. "The Big Drum and Quadrille." In *Carriacou Regatta*. St. George's, Grenada: Government Printing Office.

———. 1985. *Folklore of Carriacou*. Barbados: Coles Printery Ltd.

Delzin, Gail. 1977. "The Folk Culture of Grenada and Carriacou through Story and Song." Manuscript, St. Augustine, Trinidad: University of the West Indies.

Deren, Maya. 1953. *Divine Horsemen: The Living Gods of Haiti*. New York: Documentext McPherson and Co.

"Description of the Grenadines." 1778. Henry Strachey Papers, Band vol. 2. William L. Clements Library, University of Michigan, Ann Arbor.

Dobbins, J. D. 1986. *The Jombee Dance of Montserrat: A Study of Trance Ritual in the West Indies*. Columbus: Ohio State University Press.

Douglass, Frederick. 1987. *Narrative of the Life of Frederick Douglass*. [1845.] Rpt., *The Classic Slave Narratives*, edited by Henry Louis Gates. New York: Penguin.

Drewel, Margaret Thompson. 1992. *Yoruba Ritual*. Bloomington: Indiana University Press.

Duncan, Lucian. 1983–93. Personal communications.

Dunham, Katherine. 1983. *Dances of Haiti*. [1947.] Rpt., Los Angeles: Center for Afro-American Studies, University of California.

———. 1994. *Island Possessed*. [1969.] Rpt., Garden City, N.Y.: Doubleday.

Echewa, Obinkaram. 1985. Personal communication.

Equiano, Olaudah. 1969. *The Life of Olaudah Equiano or Gustavus Vassa, the African*. [1837.] Rpt., New York: Negro Universities Press.

Edwards, Bryan. 1793. *The History, Civil and Commercial, of the British Colonies in the West Indies*. 2 vols. London: John Stockdale.

Elder, J. D. 1966. "Evolution of the Traditional Calypso of Trinidad and Tobago: A Socio-Historical Analysis of Song." Ph.D. diss., University of Pennsylvania.

———. 1988. Conference lecture. St. Augustine, Trinidad, University of the West Indies.

Emery, Lynne Fauley. 1972. *Black Dance in the United States from 1619 to 1970*. Palo Alto, Calif.: National Press.

"Extracts from the Grenada Handbook." 1974. *Caribbean Quarterly* 20, no. 1 (March): 60–68.

Fermor, Patrick Leigh. 1950. *The Traveller's Tree: A Journey Through the Caribbean Islands*. New York: Harper and Brothers.

Fernandes, Rolando, Raul Diaz, and Laura Vilar. 1985. *Folksongs of Carriacou*. Centro de Investigacion y Desarrollo de la Musica Cubana. Havana, Cuba: EGREM Studios. Recording.

Fortes, Meyer. 1960. "Kinship and Marriage among the Ashanti." In *African Systems of Kinship and Marriage*, edited by A. R. Radcliffe-Brown and Daryll Forde. London, New York, and Toronto: Oxford University Press.

Fraginals, Manuel Moreno. 1984. *Africa in Latin America: Essays on History, Culture, and Socialization*. [1977.] Translated from the Spanish *Africa en America Latino*. New York: Holmes and Meier.

Fyfe, Christopher. 1963. *A History of Sierra Leone*. London: Oxford University Press.

Gates, Henry Louis. 1988. *The Signifying Monkey: A Theory of African-American Literary Criticism*. New York: Oxford University Press.

Glazier, Stephen D. 1983. *Marchin' the Pilgrims Home: Leadership and Decision-Making in an Afro-Caribbean Faith*. Westport, Conn.: Greenwood Press.

Greenberg, Joseph. 1966. *The Influence of Islam on a Sudanese Religion*. Seattle and London: University of Washington Press.

Grenada Almanac. 1829. Grenada: Alexander McCombie. Copy in the New York Public Library.

"Grenada Government Gazette." 1885. October 28. In the Registry, York House, St. George's, Grenada.

Guilbault, Jocelyne. 1984. "Musical Events in the Lives of the People of a Caribbean Island, St. Lucia." Ph.D. diss., University of Michigan.

———. 1993. *Zouk: World Music in the West Indies*. Chicago: University of Chicago Press.

———. 1994. "Creolité and the New Cultural Politics of Difference in Popular Music of the French West Indies." *Black Music Research Journal* 14, no. 2: 161–78.

Hall-Alleyne, Beverley. 1990. "The Social Context of African Language Continuities in Jamaica." *International Journal of Social Languages* 80: 31–40.

Hamilton, Virginia. 1986. *The People Could Fly*. New York: Knopf.

Handler, Jerome, and Charlotte Frisbie. 1972. "Aspects of Slave Life in Barbados: Music and Its Cultural Contexts." *Caribbean Studies* 11: 5–46.

Hayden, Robert. 1985. "Runagate Runagate." *Collected Poems*, edited by Frederick Glaysher. New York: Liveright.

Hazel, Clemmie Quashie. 1983. Personal communication.

Hearn, Lafcadio. 1890. *Two Years in the West Indies*. New York: Harper and Brothers.

Henney, Jeannette. 1973. "The Shakers of St. Vincent: A Stable Religion." In *Religion, Altered States of Consciousness, and Social Change*, edited by Erika Bourguignon. Columbus: Ohio State University Press.

Herskovits, Melville J. 1949. "Acculturation, the Study of Culture Contact." Sol Tax, editor. Introduction to *Acculturation in the Americas*. Chicago: International Congress of Americanists.

Herskovits, Melville J., and Frances Herskovits. 1936. *Suriname Folklore*. New York: Columbia University Press.

———. 1964. *Trinidad Village.* [1947.] Rpt., New York: Octagon.

Hill, Donald. 1973. "England I Want To Go: The Impact of Migration on a Caribbean Community." Ph.D. diss., Indiana University.

———. 1974. "More on Truth, Fact, and Tradition in Carriacou." *Caribbean Quarterly* 20, no. 1 (March): 45–59.

———. 1977. *The Impact of Migration on the Metropolitan and Folk Society of Carriacou, Grenada.* Anthropological Papers of the Museum of Natural History 54, no. 2. New York.

———. 1980. *The Big Drum and Other Ritual and Social Music of Carriacou.* Ethnic Folkways Library FE34002. Recording; includes insert.

———. 1993. *Calypso Calaloo: Early Carnival Music in Trinidad.* Gainesville: University Press of Florida.

———. In press. *"Long Time Ago": The 1962 Carriacou Field Recording of Alan Lomax.* Recording. Cambridge, Mass.: Rounder Records.

Hill, Errol. 1967. "On the Origin of the Term Calypso." *Ethnomusicology* 11, no. 3: 359–67.

———. 1972. *The Trinidad Carnival: Mandate for a National Theater.* Austin: University of Texas Press.

Hobsbawm, Eric. 1983. *The Invention of Tradition.* New York: Cambridge University Press.

Homiak, John. 1990. "Melville Herskovits: Motor Behavior and the Imaging of Afro-American Culture." *Visual Anthropology* 3: 11–29.

———. 1993. Personal communication.

———. 1995. "Dub History: Soundings in Rastafari Livity and Language. In *Rastafari and Other African-Caribbean Worldviews*, edited by Barry Chevannes. London: Macmillan Press, Ltd.

Hughes, Alister. 1966. "Non-Standard English of Grenada." *Caribbean Quarterly* 12, no. 4: 47–54.

Hurston, Zora Neale. 1973. "High John de Conquer." [1943.] Rpt. from "The American Mercury 57." In *Mother Wit from the Laughing Barrel*, edited by Alan Dundes, 450–58. Englewood Cliffs, N.J.: Prentice Hall.

———. 1983. *Tell My Horse.* [1938.] Rpt., Buena Vista, Berkeley, Calif.: Turtle Island.

Johns, Pearl. 1983. Personal communication.

Kay, Frances. 1971. *This Is Carriacou.* Trinidad: Trinidad and Tobago Printing and Packaging.

Keil, Charles. 1979. *Tiv Song.* Chicago: University of Chicago Press.

Kelly, James. 1814. *Voyage to Jamaica and Seventeen Years on That Island.* Belfast.

Kremser, Manfred, and Karl R. Wernhart. n.d. "The African Heritage in the 'Kele'— Tradition of the 'Djine'." In *Research in Ethnography and Ethnohistory of St. Lucia.* Vienna: Verlag Ferdinand Berger und Sohne.

Lashley, Cliff. 1982. "The Quashie Esthetic." *Caribe* 6, no. 1 (Spring–Summer): 27–29.

Laurence, K. O. 1982. "The Tobago Slave Conspiracy of 1810." *Caribbean Quarterly* 28, no. 3: 1–18.

Lévi-Strauss, Claude. 1983. Foreword to *Dances of Haiti* by Katherine Dunham. [1947.] Rpt., Los Angeles: Center for Afro-American Studies, University of California.

Liverpoole, Hollis. 1994. "Researching Steelband and Calypso Music in the British Caribbean and the U.S. Virgin Islands." *Black Music Research Journal* 14, no. 2: 179–201.

Logan, Wendell. 1982. "Conversations with Marjorie Whylie: Some Aspects of Religious Cult Music in Jamaica." *The Black Perspective in Music* 10, no. 1: 85–94.

Lovelace, Earl. 1997. *Salt*. New York: Persea.

Macdonald, Annette. 1962. "The Big Drum Dance of Carriacou: Its Structure and Possible Origins." Master's thesis, University of California.

Manuel, Peter. 1991. *Essays on Cuban Music: North American and Cuban Perspectives*. Lanham, Md.: University Press of America.

Marshall, Paule. 1983. *Praisesong for the Widow*. New York: Penguin.

Maurer, Bill. 1991. "Caribbean Dance: 'Resistance,' Colonial Discourse, and Subjugated Knowledges. *Nieuwe West-Indische Gids* 65, nos. 1–2: 1–26.

Mauss, Marcell. 1967. *The Gift: Forms and Functions of Exchange in Archaic Societies*. New York and London: W. W. Norton and Co.

Mayhew, Frank. 1953. "My Life." *Caribbean Quarterly* 1, nos, 1–2: 5–12.

McBurnie, Beryl. n.d. *Outlines of the Dances of Trinidad*. Trinidad: Guardian Commercial Printery.

McDaniel, Lorna. 1985. "The Stone Feast and Big Drum of Carriacou." *The Black Perspective in Music* 16, no. 5 (Spring): 179–94.

———. 1990. "The Flying Africans: Extent and Strength of the Myth in the Americas." *Nieuwe West-Indische Gids* 64, nos. 1–2: 28–40.

———. 1993. "The Concept of Nation in the Big Drum of Carriacou, Grenada." *Musical Repercussions of the 1492 encounter*, edited by Carol Robertson. Washington, D.C.: Smithsonian Institution.

———. 1994. "Memory Spirituals of the Liberated American Soldiers in Trindad's 'Company Villages'." *Black Music Research Journal* 14, no. 2 (Fall): 119–43.

Mends, Judith. 1983. Personal communication.

Meredith, Henry. 1967. *An Account of the Gold Coast of Africa: With a Brief History of the African Company*. [1812.] Rpt. Frank Cass.

Merriam, Alan. 1964. *Anthropology of Music*. Evanston, Ill.: Northwestern University Press.

Métraux, Alfred. 1972. *Voodoo in Haiti*. [1959.] Rpt., New York: Schocken Books.

Mighty Sparrow. 1984. "Grenada." On *King of the (Slinger Francisco) World*. Brooklyn, N.Y.: B's Records. Recording.

Mintz, Sidney W. 1974. *Caribbean Transformations*. Chicago: Aldine.

Mintz, Sidney W., and Richard Price. 1976. *An Anthropological Approach to the Afro-American Past: A Caribbean Perspective*. Philadelphia: Institute for the Study of Human Issues.

Montejo, Esteban. 1969. *The Autobiography of a Runaway Slave*. New York: Meridian.

Morrison, Toni. 1977. *Song of Solomon*. New York: Knopf.

———. 1987. Video. *Profile of a Writer*. London Weekend Television "South Bank Show," coproduced with RM Arts. Produced and directed by Alan Benson.

———. 1992. Response at the award of Doctor of Letters. Graduation ceremonies, University of Michigan.

Murdock, George Peter. 1965. *Culture and Society*. Pittsburgh: University of Pittsburgh Press.

Murphy, Joseph M. 1994. *Working the Spirit: Ceremonies of the African Diaspora*. Boston: Beacon Press.

Nketia, J. H. Kwabena. 1974. *The Music of Africa*. New York and London: Norton.

Nzewi, Meki. 1992. Personal communication.

Patterson, Orlando. 1973. "The Socialization and Personality Structure of the Slave." In *Slaves, Free Men, Citizens: West Indian Perspectives*, edited by Lambros Comitas and David Lowenthal. Garden City, N.Y.: Anchor-Doubleday.

Paul, Norman. 1963. *Dark Puritan: The Life and Work of Norman Paul*. Transcribed by M. G. Smith. Kingston, Jamaica: University of the West Indies.

Pearse, Andrew. 1955. "Aspects of Change in Caribbean Folk Music." *Journal of the International Folk Music Council* 7: 29–36.

——. 1956. *The Big Drum Dance of Carriacou*. Ethnic Folkways Library FE4011. Recording; includes insert.

——. 1978–79. "Music in Caribbean Popular Culture." *Revista I Interamericana* 8, no. 4: 629–39.

——. n.d. Pearse Archive, Carriacou Packet. In the author's possession, Tobago, W.I.

Pelton, Robert D. 1989. *The Trickster in West Africa: A Study of Mythic Irony and Sacred Delight*. Berkeley and Los Angeles: University of California Press.

Pollard, Velma. 1985. "Cultural Connections in Paule Marshall's *Praisesong for the Widow*." *World Literature Written in English* 25, no. 2: 285–98.

Price, Richard. 1983. *First Time: The Vision of an Afro-American People*. Baltimore and London: Johns Hopkins University Press.

Procope, Bruce. 1955. "Launching a Schooner in Carriacou." *Caribbean Quarterly* 4, no. 2: 122–31.

Puckett, Newbell Niles. 1968. *Folkbeliefs of the Southern Negro*. [1926.] Rpt., New York: Negro Universities Press.

Quevedo, Raymond. 1983. *Atilla's Kaiso: A Short History of Trinidad Calypso*. St. Augustine: Trinidad and Tobago: University of the West Indies, Department of Extra Mural Studies.

Raboteau, Albert J. 1978. *Slave Religion: "The Invisible Institution" in the Antebellum South*. New York: Oxford University Press.

Rattray, R. S. 1927. *Religion and Art in Ashanti*. London: Oxford University Press.

Robert, Paul. 1984. *Le Petit Robert: Dictionnaire Alphabetique et Analogigue de la langue Francaise*. Paris: Le Robert.

Roberts, Helen. 1926. "Possible Survivals of African Song in Jamaica." *Musical Quarterly* 12, no. 3: 340–58.

Robertson, Carol. 1983–84. Personal communications.

Sadie, Stanley. 1980. *New Grove Dictionary of Music and Musicians*. New York: Macmillan.

St. George's Chronicle. 1836. St. George's, Grenada. Copy at the American Antiquarian Society, Worchester, Mass.

St. George's Chronicle and Grenada Gazette. 1798. St. George's Grenada, Sept. 14, Nov. 13. Copies at the American Antiquarian Society, Worchester, Mass.

St. George's Chronicle and New Grenada Gazette. 1790. St. George's Grenada, July 2, Aug. 19. Copies at the American Antiquarian Society, Worchester, Mass.

St. John, Marian. 1983. Personal communication.

Schuler, Monica. 1980. *"Alas, Alas, Kongo": A Social History of Indentured African Immigration in Jamaica, 1841–1865.* Baltimore: Johns Hopkins University Press.

Seabrook, W. B. 1929. *The Magic Island.* Rahway, N.J.: Quinn and Boden, 1929.

Shelemay, Kay Kaufman. 1980. "Historical Ethnomusicology: Reconstructing Falasha Liturgical History." *Ethnomusicology* 24, no. 2: 233–58.

Simpson, George. 1962. "The Shango Cult in Nigeria and in Trinidad." *American Anthropologist* 64: 1204–19.

———. 1973. *Melville Herskovits.* New York: Columbia University Press.

———. 1977. *Religious Cults of the Caribbean: Trinidad, Jamaica, and Haiti.* Puerto Rico: Institute of Caribbean Studies, University of Puerto Rico.

———. 1978. *Black Religions in the New World.* New York: Columbia University Press.

Slade, H. Gordon. 1984. "Craigston and Meldrum Estates, Carriacou, 1769–1841." *Society of Antiquaries of Scotland* 114: 481–537.

Smith, George. 1808. *The Laws of Grenada from the Year 1763 to the Year 1805.* London: H. Bryer, Bridge Street Black Friars.

Smith, M. G. 1962a. *Kinship and Community in Carriacou.* New Haven and London: Yale University Press.

———. 1962b. "Kinship and Household in Carriacou." *Social and Economic Studies* 10, no. 4 (December): 455–77.

———. 1965. *The Plural Society in the British West Indies.* Berkeley and Los Angeles: University of California Press.

Southern, Eileen. 1997. *The Music of Black Americans.* 3d edition. New York: Norton.

"State of the Island of Carriouacou [sic]." Carriacou Census of 1775, ref ext/266 m 1607. Public Record Office, British Library, London.

Steele, Beverly. 1974. "Grenada, an Island State, Its History and Its People." *Caribbean Quarterly* 20, no. 1 (March): 5–43.

Stuckey, Sterling. 1987. *Slave Culture: Nationalist Theory and the Foundations of Black America.* New York: Oxford University Press.

———. 1994. *Going Through the Storm: The Influence of African American Art in History.* New York: Oxford University Press.

Sunshine, Catherine. 1982. *Grenada, the Peaceful Revolution.* Washington, D.C.: EPICA Task Force.

Thomas, Rt. Rev. Eudora. 1987. *A History of the Shouter Baptists in Trinidad and Tobago.* Tacariqua, Trinidad: Calaloux Publications.

Thompson, Robert Farris. 1984. *Flash of the Spirit: Afro-American Art and Philosophy.* New York: Vintage.

Turner, Lorenzo D. 1969. *Africanisms in the Gullah Dialect.* New York: Arno Press.

Turner, Victor. 1967. *The Forest of Symbols: Aspects of Ndembu Ritual.* Ithaca, N.Y.: Cornell University Press.

Valdman, Albert. 1970. *Basic Course in Haitian Creole.* Bloomington: Indiana University Press.

van Dantzig, Albert. 1980. *Forts and Castles of Ghana.* Accra: Sedco Publications.

Walker, Sheila. 1972. *Ceremonial Spirit Possession in Africa and Afro-America: Forms, Meanings, and Functional Significance for Individuals and Social Groups.* Leiden: Brill.

Warner, Keith. 1985. *Kaiso! The Trinidad Calypso: A Study of the Calypso as Oral Literature.* Washington, D.C.: Three Continents Press.

Warner-Lewis, Maureen. 1978. "Yoruba Religion in Trinidad—Transfer and Reinterpretation." *Caribbean Quarterly* 24, nos. 3–4: 18–32.

———. 1991. *Guinea's Other Sons: The African Dynamic in Trinidad Culture.* Dover, Mass.: Majority Press.

Waterman, Richard. 1943. "African Patterns in Trinidad Negro Music." Ph.D. diss., Northwestern University.

Werner, Alice. 1925. "African Mythology." In *The Mythology of All Races*, edited by John Arnott MacCulloch. Boston: Marshall Jones.

Westerman, D. 1934. *A Hausa-English Dictionary.* London: Oxford University Press.

Wilks, Ivor. 1961. *The Northern Facts in Ashanti History.* Accra: The Institute of African Studies, University College of Ghana.

———. 1975. *Asante in the Nineteenth Century: The Structure and Evolution of a Political Order.* Cambridge: Cambridge University Press.

Williams, Mervyn. 1985. "Song from Valley to Mountain: Music and Ritual among the Spiritual Baptists ("Shouters") of Trinidad." Master's thesis, Indiana University.

Williamson, Kay. 1984. "A Note on the Word 'Bekee'." *Owa ndi Igbo* 1 (June): 1.

Winer, Lise. 1986. "Socio-cultural Change and the Language of Calypso." *Nieuwe West-Indische Gids* 60, nos. 3–4: 113–48.

Wood, Donald. 1986. *Trinidad in Transition.* New York: Oxford University Press.

Index

Adams, Sugar, ii, 25, 53, 62, 99
Africans, 76; late-to-arrive, 104–5
African-type music, call-and-response, texture, 126–33, 136
Alidou, Ousseina, 47
Allert, Nevi, 141–42
Amba, 66
Anancy, Ananci, Anansi, 46, 47, 99, 121
Ancestral pantheon, 76, 167; Ahwusa Wele, 69, 169; Amma, Amba Dabia, Ambadino, Sai Amba, 60, 66, 69, 169; Anancy, 47, 169; Cromanti Cudjo, 44–46, 68; Ena, 48, 169; Ianman Igbo Lelé, 51–53, 169; Negesse Manding, 60, 169; Oko, 48–49, 169
Andrews, Estimie, xi, 11, 15, 23, 24, 81, 144
Andrews, Gentle, xi, 2
Anthropological novel, 1–3
Aruba, 134–35, 153,
Asanti song, 127; Akan, 97, 168; Akan names, 33, 64, 126; Asanti *ntoro/mogya*, 70–73, 168; Asanti port, 36, 38; "Ashante Moslems," 46; northern invasion, 37

Baptist 'Mericans, 109
Beké, bukra, mbakara, Baikie, etymology of, 62, 63, 89
Bembe, 100, 108–9, 184n.2
Benjamin, Peter, 12
Big Drum (Nation Dance): aesthetic of, 21–22, 81–82, 169; age of, 17, 152–54; Beg Pardon, Mid-night Cromanti, 22, 24, 46, 47; Bélè Kawé, 24, 135–37, 145,

163; Bongo songs, 34–36, 106, 129, 150, 153; chac-chac, 21; composition in, 59, 125, 126, 128–30, 132–35; costume of, 28; Creole, 18, 21, 25; dance classifications, 19; dance description, 25; drummers, 25, 85–86; drums, 82–98, 185; extended song forms, 135; free ring, 22; Frivolous, 18, 152–53; gwa bélè 121–23; hallecord, 81–82, 90–94, 141, 133, 138–42, 145; juba, 120, 165, 185n.6; kalenda, 129, 134, 153; kata (cutter) and boula, 88, 183–85nn.2, 3; migration and protest, 149–52, 185; Nation, 44–69, 167; ritual outline of, 20–24, 123; social structure in, 16, 20, 24–28, 71, 74, 75–77, 81, 82, 89–92, 95–97, 169; symbols in, 80, 169–70; women's wanga songs, 145–49
Bishop, Maurice, 158–59, 163–64
Blaize, Herbert, 163
Blood, 70–71, 73, 168, 183
Bowdich, T. Edward, 127

Caliste, Canute, 160, 26–27
Callaloo, 11
Calypso, 156–66; etymology of term, 156; "Grenada," 162–66
Cantique, 128
Caribbean rebellions, 31–33
Carib nation, 28–30
Carriacou: Amerindian shards in, 29, 30; Carriacou Historical Museum, 30; description of, 28–33; geography of, 6; history of, 28–34; keeping and

195

Carriacou: Amerindian shards in *(cont'd)*
friending, 91–92; lineage in, 71–74,
167, 168, 170; Marxist revolution in, 12;
multiple marriage in, 97; name of, 30;
population of, 33–34, 42; social codes
in, 168, 183n.2; well, 29–30
Carriacou Cultural Organization
(C.C.O.), 11, 14, 23
Catholic church and ritual survivals, 101;
Catholics to Trinidad, 150
Cérol, Marie-Josée, 36
Chantwell, chantuelle, chantuel, 21, 23,
143, 144
Coard, Bernard, 163–64
Concept of Nation, 36–44, 168, 170
Corion, Pofella, 11–12, 128
Cormantine, Gold Coast, images of,
38–42
Cosmogram, 78
Cosmology, 74–75; Yoruba, Kongo,
Arada, 121
Coupé Cou 24, 44, 68
Creole dance/songs, 70, 75
Creole language, 11, 17, 36, 50, 65
Creole people, 32
Creolization, 49, 115, 121, 125, 170, 183n.2
Cuba: Cubans in, 165, 166; Yorubas in,
105
Cudjo, Grantis ("the Lion"), 158
Cudjo, Simeon, 159
Cyclephonic spiral diagram, 10, 131; full
score, 131
Cyclephony, 19, 100, 130–31, 169; clef
sign, 11

Da Costa, Adrian, 79
Da Costa, Noel, 12
Da Costa, Patricia, 12
Danced Religions, 98–101, 185n.1; spirit
manifestation, trance in, 101–3, 169
Deren, Maya, 102
Diaspora, 43, 170
Douglass, Frederick, 58–59, 185n.6
Dream culture, 29, 99, 106, 169
Drums: Antillean, 85–86; ban on, 30; Big
Drum, 82, 84, 86; etymology of names,

88; Kongo, 51; Orisa, 108; and ritual
names, 82; in Spiritual Baptist service,
111; as symbol, 87, 98
Duncan, Lucian, 11, 12, 83, 133, 184n.3
Dunham, Katherine, 115, 118

Equiano, Olaudah, 50
Eshu Elegbara, Elegba, Esu, Exu,
Legba, 2, 60, 114–21, 123, 170; songs to,
184; personification of Esu by Paule
Marshall, 119
Ethnic researcher, 7
Evil eye: kokoma, obeah, 57, 106, 141;
maljo, 53–54, 186; wanga, 145–49

"Fantasi," 92
"Fixed melancholy," suicide, 168
Flight, 3–5, 168; aesthetic imagination
in, 59; and bird imagery, 81, 124;
physical flight, 32–33, 159, 162; of
spirits, 123–24; suicide as, 15–16, 99,
102, 110
Flying Africans myth, 2, 3, 4, 56; Igbo
Landing, 2, 43, 56–59, 159, 170
Food, 11, 20; parents' plate, 77, 79–80,
169
Fortune, May, 25, 8

Gairy, Eric, 165
Garvey, Marcus, 159, 162
Gates, Henry Louis, 43, 120, 116, 170
Grenada: American invasion of, 6, 158,
159; Fedon rebellion, 31–32, 159, 166;
revolution in, 12, 156, 158, 159; New
Jewel Movement in, 158, 162, 165;
George Shultz and description of, 28;
President Reagan and, 159

Haiti: banda in, 64; loa of, 51, 68, 102,
184n.1
Hayden, Robert, 3, 16
Herskovits, Melville: and acculturation,
115, 156; and Frances Herskovits on
spirit manifestations, 102
Hill, Donald, 6, 14, 78
Historical ethnomusicology, 5